Albert Zabriskie Gray

Mexico as it is

Being Notes of a recent Tour in that Country

Albert Zabriskie Gray

Mexico as it is
Being Notes of a recent Tour in that Country

ISBN/EAN: 9783337190255

Printed in Europe, USA, Canada, Australia, Japan

Cover: Foto ©Andreas Hilbeck / pixelio.de

More available books at **www.hansebooks.com**

THE AZTEC CALENDAR STONE.

MEXICO AS IT IS

BEING

NOTES OF A RECENT TOUR IN THAT COUNTRY

WITH SOME PRACTICAL INFORMATION FOR TRAVELLERS
IN THAT DIRECTION, AS ALSO SOME STUDY OF
THE CHURCH QUESTION

BY

ALBERT ZABRISKIE GRAY

AUTHOR OF "THE LAND AND THE LIFE, OR SKETCHES AND STUDIES IN PALESTINE"

NEW YORK
E. P. DUTTON & COMPANY
713 BROADWAY
1878

*Stereotyped at the Church Charity Foundation,
Brooklyn, L. I.*

TO ONE

IN WHOSE CHARACTER AND CULTURE

I RECOGNIZE THE VINDICATION

OF INTELLIGENT AND CONSCIENTIOUS TRAVEL

THIS LITTLE VOLUME

IS MOST FILIALLY

INSCRIBED

"A good land, a land of brooks of water, of fountains and depths, that spring out of valleys and hills ; a land of wheat and barley, and vines and fig-trees, and pomegranates ; a land of oil olive, and honey ; a land wherein thou shalt eat bread without scarceness, thou shalt not lack anything in it ; a land, whose stones are iron, and out of whose hills thou mayest dig brass."—DEUT. viii. 7, 8, 9.

CONTENTS.

CHAPTER	PAGE
I.—Prefatory Chapter	9
II.—New York to Vera Cruz	17
III.—Vera Cruz to Orizaba	27
IV.—Orizaba to the City of Mexico	35
V.—The City of Mexico	44
VI.—The Environs of the City of Mexico	56
VII.—The Environs of the City of Mexico *(continued)*	65
VIII.—The Environs of the City of Mexico *(continued)*	71
IX.—The Environs of the City of Mexico *(concluded)*	81
X.—Puebla and Cholula	91
XI.—Cholula *(continued)*	103
XII.—How we tried to get to Xalapa	113
XIII.—The Church in Mexico	127

"One circumstance must be observed by all who travel in Mexican territory. There is not one human being or passing object to be seen that is not in itself a picture, or which would not form a good subject for the pencil. The Indian women, with their plaited hair, and little children slung to their backs, their large straw hats, and petticoats of two colors—the long strings of arrièros with their loaded mules, and swarthy, wild-looking faces—the chance horseman who passes with his sarape of many colors, his high ornamented saddle, Mexican hat, silver stirrups, and leathern boots, this is picturesque. Salvator Rosa and Hogarth might have travelled here to advantage, hand-in-hand; Salvator for the sublime, and Hogarth taking him up where the sublime became the ridiculous."

From " Life in Mexico," by Madame C— de la B——.

PREFACE.

A PART of this little volume first appeared as letters in the Hartford "CHURCHMAN." The completion of the series, and their presentation in book-form, was urged upon the writer by kind friends. He complies with their wishes the more readily when he reflects that possibly some service may be rendered to those intending to visit our fair "Sister Republic."

This service may be increased by embodying in these prefatory remarks some practical information and hints with regard to the character of the country and the pre-requisites of travel and residence therein.

Mexico is a republic, modeled very much upon the Constitution of the United States. It consists of twenty-seven states, one territory, and what is called the Federal District, which includes the capital.

The total area is more than twelve hundred thousand square miles, and contains a population of about nine millions, of which a large proportion is aboriginal Aztec blood.

The principal exports are gold and silver, in which the country possesses inexhaustible wealth. It also produces coffee, tobacco, sugar, indigo, vanilla, hides, dye-woods, fruits, etc. etc. There is no richer region in the world; very few lands are as rich in all that constitutes material prosperity and promise; and this, of course, is largely due to the fact of its comprising, in its comparatively limited area, almost every soil and every temperature. The great range of the Sierra Madre runs through the whole country, and thus affords a wonderful variety of vegetation.

In the Tierra Caliente of the coast you have the fecund and feverish tropics. On the mountain slopes and plateaux you can enjoy a climate of perfect salubrity and refreshment, and find growing, side by side, the corn and the banana, the palm and the tobacco; and in the still higher regions—of the capital and elsewhere—you will sleep all the year under a blanket, while feasting every day on the lusciousness, brought by a few hours of rail from the burning plains seven thousand feet below. And finally, to complete the charm, you have, rising above all and ever refreshing, the majestic peaks of Orizava, Popocatepetl and Istacyhuatl—with their eternal snows — more than fifteen thousand feet above the sea. You must consequently take with you some variety of clothing, in preparation for all these temperatures, never forgetting the overcoat and rug for evening and night, always remembering that it is better to have too much than too little.

The history of the country is soon sketched, though do not forget to take with you a small edition of Prescott's charming narrative, as also a copy of Madame Calderon's fascinating letters, if you can procure it. Any one of the diaries of Cortes, Bernal Diaz, or of the histories of Clavigero and Herrera would add immensely to the interest of a visit to Mexico, while violating, of course, a canon of travel in incumbrance.

We all know something about the earliest historical inhabitants—the Toltecs and the Aztecs. What

New Yorker has quite forgotten the thrill of interest with which he inspected "the Aztec children," exhibited many years ago by the indefatigable showman, and classed in memory somewhat promiscuously with the mysterious "What is it," the uncomfortable twins of Siam, and innumerable other *lusi naturæ* of the age?

Prescott tells us, in his romantic style, of how these semi-civilized Aztecs, under their gorgeous king, were cruelly conquered and completely subjugated by the ruthless valor of Cortes and his little band of braves, and then we learn how at once decrepid Spain began to feast and fatten on the exuberant land, enriching her Court, her Church, her commerce in the life-blood of a noble race, whose souls' salvation she ever professed as her first aim!

The Spaniards retained full possession of the country until the beginning of this century, when already a large, mixed, so-called Mexican population existed, essentially Spanish in character, but imbued with many of the revolutionary ideas of that day, which were soon precipitated by the reckless policy of the mother country into revolt.

Its first leader was **a priest named Hidalgo**, who soon sealed his patriotism with his blood.

The country was **declared independent** in 1813, and has **continued in a pitiable state of unrest and warfare**—both **internal and** external—ever since. **The internecine** struggles have been principally **due to** the unprincipled ambition of such men as Iturbide and Santa Anna, and **alas, Mexico** has been blessed with but few rulers, who, **like** Juarez, **seem to have** comprehended **the great** principles of **their blood-bought** Constitution! The Spaniards **were not** finally **expelled till** 1829, the same **year in which** slavery **was abolished**.

The **unhappy country has suffered from** several invasions. The first of any importance was the war with the United States, which ended with the indemnified cession by **Mexico of Texas,** Upper California, etc., in 1848. In 1862 the allied powers of England, France and Spain attempted to obtain financial satisfaction from the republic, and later, under the armed auspices **of** France, Maximilian was declared **Emperor.** His short but brilliant reign — three years of tragic struggle—set in clouds and blood.

He was captured and executed in June, 1867. The country resumed its republican Constitution, and enjoyed a period of comparative peace and prosperity under the presidential rule of Juarez. It is only of late that a complete revolution has again been attempted; and to-day we have the unedifying spectacle of the recent and able President Lerdo de Tejada a powerless exile, the brave but revolutionary General Diaz occupying his seat, while a third aspirant, the ex-Chief-Justice Iglesias is also among "the outs," and engaged in issuing pronunciamentos at a safe distance.

It is estimated that the poor, groaning country has suffered a change of rule, on an average, once a year since its independent existence.

With regard, again, to a few practical hints for those intending to visit the country, let us briefly say: The best time for a tour in Mexico is the winter—the safest from fevers—though at any season it is best not to linger any longer than absolutely necessary upon the coast. You can go by way of New Orleans—making a shorter sea-trip—or from New York via Havana, in which case a passport is required. American, English, or French gold will take you anywhere, and give a comfortable premium besides, leaving you under the pleasant impression that you are making money all the time. But of course you will take a letter of credit, which, following the above premium rule, will load your pockets and trunks with Mexican bullion, and keep you somewhat nervous in brigand neighborhoods.

Which leads to one final and friendly advice: take no nervousness with you. Take patience, good-temper, charitable judgment, considerate kindness—take, in short, your Christianity with you, and you cannot fail to have a most delightful time.

All travellers may be classified under two heads: the men who have been everywhere, passed their best years in genteel wanderings, and yet have never really seen anything, and can only be aroused to enthusiasm by the discussion of such a question as the comparative merits of *table d'hôtes;* and again, those who cannot take a turn down the street without a fruitful harvest of observation, and to whom one stroll amid the stimulating scenes of a foreign land is almost an education

To the former a trip to Mexico would be simply adding another—perhaps a somewhat stranger feather to the cap of voyager conquest and conceit—to the latter it would prove a feast forever.

II.

NEW YORK TO VERA CRUZ.

IT may be said to require a winter trip southward to appreciate the extent and advantages of our own country. To leave New York in a winter storm, and in sixty-five hours to glide into a sister city revelling in spring sunshine and flowers—in other words, to travel 1,500 miles in order to take a steamer from New Orleans—makes one realize what a wonderful land we live in! A five miles walk in the Mammoth Cave shows us again that even "under the earth," American nature keeps up her grand scale; and a visit to the motley Louisiana Legislature convinces one that in radical changes American humanity is resolved not to be below the mark.

New Orleans is a fair city, and deserves a better lot than she has found in these latter days; but we rejoiced to remark a hopeful spirit in her better people, and a conviction that the era of "carpet-bag" misrule is nearly past.

Certainly no one can stroll through the streets and squares of her old French quarter without yielding to a charm, that carries one dreamily over land and sea to many a distant scene and delightful hour of wandering in regions so little known to the rushing American—the south of France. The old cathedral and the buildings about it—formerly occupied by the French authorities—are alone worth a visit from any distance. We have nothing like them elsewhere in "the States." The square around which they stand is kept in that precise French style which in a land like ours, has at least the striking attraction of contrast.

And the people themselves—I mean of course the Creole part of them—seem to cling to their former nationality. We were informed that many of them are never seen out of the French quarter, where indeed French names and French signs meet you at every step.

And, before leaving the old city, we would speak a word of almost unqualified commendation with regard to its principal hotel. We were told that the St. Charles is "run" with but little profit to its proprietors and managers, and they certainly deserve great credit for the excellence of everything connected with it. To one seeking a mild winter climate, and who has suffered from the discomforts of Florida and other parts of the South, this word may be of service. We speak of Florida as we knew some parts of it two or three years ago.

The steamers from New Orleans to Vera Cruz are of the well-known "Alexandre" line, starting from New York. Compared with our trans-Atlantic steamers, they are small and only tolerably comfortable. The great drawback to the voyage is their stopping at intermediate ports, and thus giving the nauseated traveller two unnecessary days. There is nothing to see or to do at these ports. You lie off in the open roadstead, two or three miles from shore, and of course roll most unhappily at the slightest suggestion of Boreas. You have hardly time to go ashore, and indeed are tantalized by the distant and inviting verdure of the Mexican tropics. What is most urgently demanded for the tourist in that direction is a first-class line of steamers running directly from New Orleans, or from New York to New Orleans, and return, stopping only at Havana and Vera Cruz.

There is not a decent harbor in the Gulf of Mexico. As our good captain remarked, 'If your vessel does come to any grief, you would hardly know what port to make for.'

The city of Vera Cruz—the main port of the republic on the Atlantic side—lies on the open coast, only protected from the "wild waves," by some merciless reefs and the picturesque island fort of San Juan d'Ulloa, where the Spaniards under Cortes first landed. As is the fashion at this season of the Mexican year, we arrived in "a Norther." But fortune, as we know, ever "favors the brave," and a brave man did we have in our captain. He is said to be the only man of the Line who can do what he did that rough morning. Being a pilot as well, he took his vesssl right in between the reefs and through the gale, and brought her to her anchorage without a scratch. It was a beautiful and thrilling thing to see. There were but four vessels in the anchorage; among them, as we were informed, lay half of the Mexican navy, viz., two small, neat-looking vessels, about the size of our revenue cutters.

Once landed—not without a surf-drenching, however—at the Customs quay, you are met and surrounded at once with the sights and scenes, the novelties and oddities of a widely-differing civilization.

The old town of "the Conquerors," fondly named by them Villa Rica de la Vera Cruz, has been much abused by many disgusted travellers, arriving and departing from its sea-beaten and sand-girt walls, and we must admit that, with its glaring whitewash, and open street-drains, and clouds of scavenger buzzards, its thousand smells, and sickliest reputation, it may be not inaptly compared to a "whited sepulchre;" but withal we have rarely seen a town more picturesque—well and compactly built—one of the few cities left in North America that have retained their walls; its many domes and glaring colors giving a semi-Oriental aspect to its architecture, and its patioed houses, the tropical vegetation of its squares and alameda, adding a charm to the whole, only to be experienced in those fair and fatal southern lands.

But we would hasten to qualify the last alarming adjective by remarking, that during the winter months, or in other words, the prevalence of "Northers," the terrible scourge of the "Vomito" is comparatively little felt, and scarcely to be dreaded. Wherefore remember, impatient and irritated traveller, tossed and tumbled and literally thrown ashore by the force of whistling wind and regardless surf, that this very discomfort is thy salvation! Without these forcible reminders of northern inclemency, Vera Cruz would be all but uninhabitable, and thy curious visit utterly out of the question.

As it was, we were obliged to remain in the quaint old city about a week altogether, and were assured we ran no risk in doing so, though we believe it is essential to exercise the greatest caution at all seasons. Nothing can be more interesting than a stroll through the straight and narrow streets, for the Spaniards seem to have learned at least one good lesson from the natives, in laying out their towns with great regularity.

Looking into dark, and we must add, rather dirty rooms, you will see the native women on their knees most industriously kneading their tortillas, using the same curious low, inclined stone stand, on which their mothers worked long before the historic era of the Montezumas. Indeed, in features, dress, and customs, the several millions of native Indians seem to have undergone as little change as the desert Arabs. The modifications are all seen in the two or three millions of mixed blood, which are in fact the restless, revolutionary and governing race of the country.

But to pass down the sun-baked street a little farther, let us pause for a moment to examine the workings of this cigar-factory. Here are half a dozen or more of men and boys diligently and deftly selecting, rolling, pointing, etc., from not very tempting heaps of tobacco rags, finishing off those neat ends with some very doubtful-looking grease, and one of these individuals, (only one, I am happy to say) using occasionally his tongue in the operation. A little farther on we come upon the washing-square, and, as usual in Southern lands, we find a very picturesque scene.

A well-arranged and clean-looking series of troughs, under cover, and filled with pure looking water, and the whole enlivened by the merry laugh and jest of the many brown and bright-eyed and busy *lavanderas*.

And, speaking of water, we cannot omit allusion to an establishment of baths we visited, one of the most luxurious places we ever saw, almost fulfilling the ideal of "marble halls" and tropic glory. It is near the impressive old monastic building and creditable collection of the Public Library.

There is one thing in which Vera Cruz is not deficient, and indeed, it is about the only article of which Mexico seems to enjoy an *embarras de richesses*, viz., churches. The disestablishment of the Church and the confiscation of ecclesiastical property has, of course, rendered it impossible to sustain the extraordinary number of churches and convents with which the generation of Còrtes and their successors have covered the land. It is a common thing to find of several in an urban or rural neighborhood, the half abandoned. How they still maintain so many is a mystery, and yet not much of one, after all, to him who understands somewhat the workings of Rome.

The cathedral of Vera Cruz is an imposing edifice, both externally and internally. The external effect is rendered not a little *bizarre* by the black mass of carrion birds, to which we have before alluded, and which, especially toward nightfall, are seen to settle on domes and pinnacles, and indeed on every salient summit; and weirdly significant, several of the stronger ones pushing their way to a perch on the highest point of the cross itself.

Internally the church is large, and generally plain, but about its principal altars rich in precious metals. Here will we begin to realize a little of that fabulous wealth, with which the *conquistadores* sought, for their souls' sake, tarnished by so many crimes, to buy a churchly indulgence; but a large part of which the too willing Church has been unable to preserve from the necessities of later and less scrupulous criminality.

Before leaving Vera Cruz, and for the sake of common charity, let me warn brother tourists against a hotel, into which they may, by accident, stray, viz., the "Hotel des Diligencias." It seems to be managed a good deal upon the principle of the "golden egg" story. Its rooms are among the best in town, and its situation one of the finest, but there is an evident and painful intention on the part of the female proprietor to make the most of the disadvantages under which you labor in claiming her hospitality.

And this leads us to remark more seriously that the drainage arrangements of this hotel, as indeed of almost every house and every place we saw in Mexico, are simply execrable and deadly. If no other malarious reason existed, this horror of filth would be enough of itself to breed a pestilence. Decency would forbid further details of the nuisance, but decency makes it a duty to protest and to warn against an evil which must be impairing so widely and so deeply the health and prospects of the nation.

III.

VERA CRUZ TO ORIZABA.

THE city of Vera Cruz lies on a sandy and forbidding stretch of coast, but with nothing in its apparent character to indicate the causes of its great unhealthiness. The original town of Villa Rica was built a little to the north of the present site, and we believe the fatal *vomito* was not known till some time after the conquest. There seems to be no topographical or other reason why the city—the main seaport of the Republic, and indeed the key to its whole Atlantic coast—should have been erected where it is. There are several other points more sheltered, and in every way favorable; but such selections, as the student of history soon learns, are more often made from superstitious or traditional than from physical reasons. It is distant about two hundred and eighty miles from the City of Mexico.

Modern and mainly English enterprise has constructed a railway over that distance, which may be called one of the wonders and delights of the world; its eighteen hours of transit, however, being less wonderful than the story told of Montezuma, that his table was regularly supplied with fish caught in the Gulf the day before! This railway to the capital may be said to traverse almost every clime, showing the unparalleled advantages of the country. From the tropical exuberance of the *Tierre Caliente* to the temperate slopes of Orizaba, and the fertility of the Mexican *plateau*, the traveller passes with amazing facility and impression, the only drawback to the journey being found in the fact that the spirit of the Mexican age has seen fit to import for the benefit of the above-mentioned traveller the most uncomfortable of old-fashioned American cars.

As to the hour of starting, we fancy there will be but one voice among all respectable readers of this chapter. It was simply heathenish. The one passenger-train from Vera Cruz to the city of Mexico leaves about midnight,* the sole advantage to the tourist being that it makes his passage over the torrid plains more comfortable; but of course he must lose his first fascinating impression of their luxuriant beauty.

And here comes the first startling reminder as to the insecurity of the country. One entire car is devoted to the escort of fifty troops, whose duty it is to see you safely through the regions of lawlessness and rebellion—either term doing as well as the other!

Your fellow-passengers consist of a few adventurous spirits like yourself, who, tired of ordinary humdrum travel, would willingly incur a little risk to visit "the halls of the Montezumas," and, besides them, a not very prepossessing number of the present native occupants of those so-called halls. With their dusky faces, their gorgeous *sombreros*, and other *caballero* dress, and their incessant cigarettes, we must observe they do not form the most agreeable addition to the company, and we could not but

---

* Or rather, left, at the time of our visit.

regret to observe how soon some of our American compatriots, who would feel most aggrieved to be denied the designation of gentlemen, adopted the rude and vulgar custom of smoking in cars and dining-rooms, regardless of the presence of ladies. In such a motley company we rode through the long, dark hours of the tropic night, solaced indeed by the spicy breaths and breezes that came through the open windows to our dreamy sense.

It was six hours to Orizaba, and from the glare of Vera Cruz, from the gloom of our night's ride, we found ourselves in the early morn amid a scene of such marvellous beauty as was itself much more than worth our thousands of miles of journeying over land and sea. It was a revelation of natural glory. It was Switzerland beside Andalusia, Norway by the Delta, England and Italy side by side. Above us towered grand mountains, bold-peaked, yet clad in living green, until their loftiest summit, known as Orizaba, eternally white with snow, reached an elevation far beyond the highest point of Europe.

The city itself is situated about four thousand feet above the sea, and thus enjoys a perfect climate all the year round, neither sultry, as it is lower down at Cordova and Vera Cruz, nor almost exhaustingly rarefied as it is on the higher plateau of Mexico. On the surrounding plains and slopes grow luxuriantly the products of almost every clime—truly " a land of corn and wine and oil, wherein thou mayest eat bread without scarceness, and out of whose hills thou mayest dig brass." It was everywhere like a garden of beauty and fertility, with the quaint old city nestled most picturesquely and invitingly in the midst.

We soon found ourselves in an exceedingly comfortable hotel, and were thus enabled to recommend Orizaba as one of the most attractive winter resorts we have ever had the delight of visiting. Certainly, when considering the climate, the scenery, the comfort and reasonableness of living, we can hardly recall any spot in either the East or West so advantageous. A walk through the clean and regular streets reveals all the charming characteristics of Spanish life— the large, low, iron-grated windows, with dark-hued *señoras* idly looking out, and glimpses beyond of sunny *patios*, luxuriant with flowers and plashing fountains. And then the old churches, glaring and crumbling without, tawdry within, a brace of not unhappy-looking cripples at the door, and inside the usual assortment of mantillaed dames and mumbling beggars, a drowsiness and a dreaminess of both faith and climate investing the whole with a charm which no soul, with any music, can resist.

Stop with me a moment in this old lane leading out from the suburbs. It is narrow, neglected, grass-grown. On each side stands a half-ruined church or monastery, nearly overrun with tropic growth. And so all along, as far as the eye can reach, extends this most exuberant and radiant vegetation—a vista of natural glory, animated with the continual passing to and fro of the natives in their picturesque national costumes. The vanity displayed by some of the young *caballeros* is so genuine, and, we may say, unaffected, as to be simply amusing. Both their horses and themselves are tricked out in the gayest style from head to foot; their *sombreros* like a parasol in size, and glittering with gold or silver, a man being known in Mexico very much by the *façon* of his hat. They are all more or less armed, and the richer ones followed by mounted servants, who are the fainter reproductions of themselves. Their fiery little horses seem the perfection of docility, speed, endurance, and fidelity. We saw one whose rider was hopelessly drunk, and we hardly knew which more to admire, the wonderful way the poor sot kept his seat, or the gentle forbearance with which the nobler brute accommodated himself to his master's condition.

But amidst all this animation of scene and character, we could not be blind to the sad evidences of national instability and decay. The dilapidations are from intestine feud; the neglected churches show the lapse of faith, the lounging *señoras* and the dandy *caballeros* mark the lack of higher aim and ambition, which is confirmed by the abject appearance of the Indian peasantry; and altogether, our afternoon's walk in Orizaba leaves us with impressions as sad of its humanity as they are fascinating of its site and scenery.

MOUNTAIN SCENERY ON THE TABLE-LAND IN MEXICO.

IV.

ORIZABA TO THE CITY OF MEXICO.

IT was on a perfect Spring morning that we reluctantly left Orizaba for the City of Mexico—a sky of glorious intensity, setting off the snowy diadem of Orizaba's "breathless peak," the air an elixir of health and exhilaration, and every tropic blade and leaf shimmering in the early dawn and dew.

We were ever ascending — by gradually steeper grades, till, on the mountain side, it became 212 feet to the mile — passing through fertile valleys and by sparkling streams, near high-walled *haciendas*, by meek-looking herds of cattle, and quite as meek-looking Indian peasants, interspersed with much fiercer-looking Mexican *rancheros* or other picturesque horsemen.

Soon began for us the enjoyment of magnificent views. We were literally climbing up a mountain more than 8,000 feet high, by a zigzag way, that we would call wonderful for a diligence road in the Alps of Europe, but which by rail, becomes a stupendous feat of engineering. Hewn out of the mountain side, spanning terrible ravines by iron bridges, over which you look into an almost sheer thousand feet or more, the propulsion by a double-engine locomotive of marvellous power, and everything conducted with that perfect order and precision, which gives such confidence everywhere in English management, this railway can certainly be considered one of the wonders of the world; and the many millions of its cost do not seem very much after you have seen the difficulties, and the way in which they have been surmounted. The importance and value of its construction is shown in the fact, as stated by an official, that its earnings for one month—January of this year—were $560,000.

But we began to speak of the glorious views as we ascended, of fertile valleys, cultivated plains, a changing, yet ever luxuriant vegetation, here and there a town or hamlet with its characteristic variegation of color, and conspicuous church-towers and campaniles and all around the beautiful mountain peaks, and all and everything rejoicing in the ceaseless summer sun!

Then we would creep through narrow defiles, with crystal streams brawling happily beside us, and the rich mountain flora glistening in the morning dew.

The air was bracingly keen. It was difficult to believe we had just left the sultry tropics. It completed the revival of Orizaba; when we reached the station at the summit of the pass, called Boca del Monte, we were in a condition that boded ill for the breakfast larder.

But be it said, to the credit of whomsoever it concerns, that we found here, as everywhere at the eating-places on this road and its branches, a most abundant and satisfactory provision, and at reasonable charges—a provision that should shame nearly all the American part of the way from New York to the Mexican capital.

Such coffee, we fancy, never entered the wildest dreams of a railroad caterer in the United States; and, indeed, throughout Mexico we may say, the coffee is a beverage of elysian delight. We felt we never could get enough of it, but were obliged to content ourselves with three times a day; and such are its properties, as perhaps also of the climate, that it does not seem to affect you in the least beyond satisfactory stimulation.

And while speaking of the railway travel in Mexico, it would be more than remiss not to allude to the perfect courtesy and attention of all connected with it. The principal employés of the road are English and American, and it seemed a delight to them to do anything in their power to facilitate our plans and pleasure—thereby furnishing an example, and perhaps also affording a warning to railway officials elsewhere, the world over.

And we cannot forbear, also, in this connection, very pardonably we trust, mentioning the case of one, with whom at this mountain station we became very pleasantly acquainted, which shows indeed how honest industry can make its way anywhere, even in such a disordered country as Mexico.

A man of humble origin, an Irish Roman Catholic, but of strong, sturdy character, he came to Mexico as a poor laborer, and is now, only a few years later, in an important and confidential position of inspection, and in receipt of a salary of several thousand dollars. Truly the world is wide, and "there is always room in the front ranks!"

After leaving Boca del Monte, the exact elevation of which is said to be 8,326 feet above the sea, there is a slight descent until you come to the level of the great plateau or valley of Mexico. The elevation of the capital itself is stated as about 7,500 feet.

The change is very marked from the bold mountain region—so rich in vegetation from its greater moisture—to the immense and almost monotonous plain, looking at this dry season of the year painfully parched.

But its fertility, notwithstanding, seems unbounded, producing frequent and vast crops of barley, corn, etc., and as you near the City of Mexico, being given up almost entirely to the cultivation of the *pulque* plant, the commercial value of which may be estimated from the fact that it pays in freightage to the railway company $1,000 a day.

There are mysteries of all kinds in this world of ours, and not among the least of them is this national Mexican beverage of *pulque*—to the natives what claret is to the Frenchman, beer to the German, ale to the Englishman, and we might remark, what whiskey sadly is to the American.

But all these liquids are, to say the least, not repulsive in taste; whereas *pulque*, to the uninitiated, is of all sour things the most disgusting.

We are ready to admit that it may be, in moderation, innocuous and even wholesome; indeed, we saw but very few men improperly under its influence, and they were only stupidly helpless, never violent.

We can believe also that, prepared specially for the richer classes, it may taste no worse than an ordinary condition of "spoiledness"—all this we can readily suppose, and we may conclude its consideration with the charitable supposition that, being cast, with a pig-skin full of it, upon a desert rock in the Pacific, might perhaps lead to a more grateful appreciation of one of the possibilities of nature!

It was most interesting, as we rode along, to notice the *haciendas* and towns near our line of travel, or far away upon the mountain slopes.

The former were like villages in themselves, each

containing a church and quite a population of servants and retainers. The aristocratic owners rarely visit them, and more rarely reside in them. Indeed, this would increase the chances of attack from the ubiquitous brigands, who have an uncomfortable way in this republican country of carrying off a rich man to their dens and keeping him there until a good, fat ransom has been paid; and happy the Dives who returns in full possession of all his members!

These *haciendas* are all, therefore, well walled and fortified, and carry on at times very respectable battles and sieges. They are usually situated on immense estates, and even under all these adverse circumstances, yield great revenues to their owners.

The larger hamlets and towns are very picturesque and attractive, *at a distance;* but are said to be, or until recently to have been, very nests of robbery and crime.

In fact, at every station of our road, we observed a body of volunteer cavalry drawn up in brilliant array to protect us from the possible raids of neighboring *banditti.*

The moralizing reader may be interested to learn the sequel, if not the conclusion, to this formidable display of friendliness to the government and ourselves.

As we returned over this way a few weeks later, all these brave and patriotic protectors had become banditti themselves, or had "pronounced," which is about the same thing!

The tropic day was waning towards its glowing close as we neared "the city of the Montezumas."

As if to welcome us befittingly, great, gorgeous banks of clouds, relieved by every delicateness of celestial hue, stretched their regal canopy from mountain-top to mountain-top again.

Twin queens of tropic peaks, Popocatepetl and Iztacihuatl, flushed a roseate greeting to our stranger footsteps! Glorious in elevation, (being some 3,000 feet higher than the monarch of all Europe's mountains,) crowned with everlasting snows, a perpetual feast of refreshment to tropic eyes, standing as serenely proud and pure as when, in the centuries past, filed between them the war-worn band of Cortes, and later, passed beneath them the invincible army of Scott, and the veteran troops of Maximilian—majestic peaks indeed, which the reverent eye can never, and would never lose while in this fair and fertile valley of the Aztecs!

Between them and ourselves, as we approached, lay the quiet waters of Tezcuco, set in the peaceful plain, and recalling so much of thrilling interest in the romantic annals of Anahuac.

The city itself came upon us almost suddenly, protected as it is by nearer hills, and shaded by a rich and grateful foliage in parks, *paseos*, and suburbs.

It was already the dusk of evening, and in a gentle "April shower," that we alighted from our railway carriages to seek hospitality and rest in this once imperial city of an ever mysterious race, a city and a race vested with the glamor of a history stranger than the strangest romance.

> "Thou art beautiful,
> Queen of the Valley! thou art beautiful!
> Thy walls, like silver, sparkle to the sun;
> Melodious wave thy groves; thy garden sweets
> Enrich the pleasant air; upon the lake
> Lie the long shadows of thy towers."
> *Southey's Madoc.*

V.

THE CITY OF MEXICO.

VIEW IN THE SQUARE IN THE CITY OF MEXICO.

THE first impression of the City of Mexico is somewhat disappointing to the mind fresh from the romantic pages of Prescott, but a more deliberate observation will appreciate its unsurpassed picturesqueness and advantages of site, and confirm the general verdict, that it is the best-built Spanish city on the American continent.

There are people, indeed, who are always disappointed; who visit Venice, Rome and Naples, and grumble over continual disenchantment. Their ideas of history seem mostly a compound of popular novels, flavored with "the Arabian Nights," and who, therefore, feel quite lost in the present sombre silence of the Grand Canal, in the dilapidations of the Seven-hilled City, and in the ineffaceable odors of what was so recently the Bomba Bourbon capital.

And thus with Mexico—the city of Montezuma and of Cortes, and gilded forever by the genius of one of America's greatest historians. It is, perhaps, a disappointment to find so few vestiges of an empire, which appears to have vied in luxury and pomp, in all the appliances and arts of living, with any contemporaneous nation of the older world.

The selfish, ruthless greed of the conquerors seems to have swept almost everything away. The very worst thing that can be said against the Aztecs—to wit, their human sacrifices—pales beside the subsequent atrocities, both of Church and State, committed against these heathen Indians under the name of Christianity!

We say, therefore, that, considering the generally unprincipled and reckless character of these Spanish adventurers, the intelligent traveller must be agreeably surprised to see what a city they founded, and how wisely in rebuilding they followed some of the best ideas of their victim converts.

The new city was built upon the lines of the old, destroyed in the last furious battles of the almost exterminating war. The streets are laid out with remarkable width and regularity, but they do not extend to the dimensions of the Aztec capital. Prosperous as is the present city, it is smaller than the old by very many thousands of population,* and long ancient avenues are seen stretching away from it in every direction, which formerly were teeming with life and industry.

Undoubtedly the great charm of the city has been

---

* The present population is about 200,000, we believe.

lost in the subsidence of the lake, which once extended into the street-canals, and formed the gorgeous floating gardens of Aztec wealth and romance. At present the lake is a league distant from the capital, and, unruffled by any commerce, must present a depressing contrast with the day when it was alive with Indian crafts of every kind and purpose.

The centre of all interest in the capital is, of course, its great square, a large part of which is laid out as a beautiful park. On one side stands the cathedral, one of the largest, if not the largest place of worship on this continent, and occupying the site of the great *Teocalli* of the Aztecs. With regard to this *Teocalli* or temple, we are told "that within its enclosure were five hundred dwellings. That its hall was built of stone and lime, and ornamented with stone serpents. We hear of its four great gates, fronting the four cardinal points; of its stone-paved court; great stone stairs, and sanctuaries dedicated to the gods of war; of the square destined for religious dances, and the colleges for the priests, and seminaries for the priestesses; of the horrible temple, whose door was an enormous serpent's mouth; of the temple of mirrors and that of shells; of the house set apart for the emperor's prayers; of the consecrated fountains, the birds kept for sacrifice, the gardens for the holy flowers, and of the terrible towers composed of the skulls of the victims—strange mixture of the beautiful and the horrible! We are told that five thousand priests chanted night and day in the Great Temple, to the honor and in the service of the monstrous idols, who were anointed thrice a day with the most precious perfumes; and that of these priests the most austere were clothed in black, their long hair dyed with ink, and their bodies anointed with the ashes of burnt scorpions and spiders; their chiefs were the sons of kings."

The present cathedral is an exceedingly impressive building, and fixed upon one side is the huge, mysterious "calendar stone," weighing many tons, and transported from its distant quarry by appliances which have equally baffled the best antiquarian scholars of our day.

The interior presents nothing very remarkable beyond its immensity. The choir stands singularly near the opposite end from the high altar and apse, and is connected with the former by a railed passage-way, which rails were once, as we are told, of solid silver — long since, however, devoted to political necessities! There is some fine woodwork in the choir, and there are a few tolerable paintings. The sacristy is a noble room, and the marble arrangements for priestly ablution are remarkably handsome and complete. In one of the several visits we paid to this cathedral, upon a Lenten Sunday, we found a large and devout congregation.

Another side of the square is taken up with the palace, now occupied by the President with as much enjoyment, doubtless, as by any of his Imperial predecessors. It is a long, low, white building, plain even to shabbiness, but good enough, we suppose, for a bachelor chief!* The hall of ambassadors, or of State receptions, is interesting from its life-size portraits of Mexican rulers, from the Independence. A remarkable fact of these men is that several were priests, and nearly all educated under Jesuit influence. Undoubt-

---

* Lerdo was still President at the time of our visit.

edly the most of them were men of lofty patriotism. Hidalgo, one of the first to lead the revolted Mexicans, was a village curate, whose soul was fired by the injustice and oppression of Spain. Juarez, one of the noblest of them all, was a pure-blooded Indian, who, with all his "opportunities," died a poor man — one good lesson of little, despised Mexico to her great, Pharisaic sister in the North! Lerdo, the present ruler, is an educated, shrewd, and somewhat unscrupulous man, resorting, perhaps from political necessity, to some means of government, which make the name of republic a farce. During our stay in the capital, he recruited his army by sending a column of troops to sweep through the streets, impressing the poor and respecting the rich. The present revolution is partly due, we fear, to this arbitrariness, though we must recognize that the embers of such disorder seem ever smouldering in this unhappy land, and can only be extinguished by the consistency of a purer faith and a wider, truer education.

To return again to the palace. It was sadly significant to observe upon many magnificent vases and other ornaments the cipher of Maximilian, which the republican succession could not remove without damage, and which therefore has been very sensibly allowed to remain. In the armory of the palace we were shocked to see the stand of arms with which the poor, well-meaning, but misguided monarch was shot; and our feelings were not much relieved by observing in the same hall a number of tattered American flags, captured in the Mexican war.

On the opposite side of the square from the palace stands one of the most interesting buildings remaining of the older city. It is the palace built and occupied for a time by Cortes. It is a plain, substantial edifice, built, as customary, about a large court, and now used as the government "Monte Pio" or pawn-broking establishment. Here, if your eyes are open and your pocket able, you can often pick up objects of interest and value, *bric-a-brac*, in short, "for a song." There is everything, indeed, from a coach to a ring, displayed in the spacious halls and rooms, and so with little effort or expense, you may succeed some day in purchasing a bauble of the conquerors. In fact the whole country is a mine of interest for the antiquary and the scholar, for collectors of all kinds and travellers of all aims.

The interest of sight-seeing is enhanced by the fact that you must be your own "Murray" and "Baedeker." No slavish absorption in a printed page—so often at the expense of the object itself; no servile following in the footsteps of an illiterate *valet de place*. There is no such thing as a guide-book known in the whole free land of Mexico! By dint of much search and persuasion we succeeded in securing the services of an elderly colored man, who had gone to Mexico as a body-servant to one of Scott's officers, and who, through much tribulation, had been able to settle there. He gave us cheerfully the benefit of his linguistic and other advantages, but I verily believe we taught him much more than he had ever begun to suspect about the city and environs, before we were through with him. And thus we found out that there was a picture gallery, with some very poor pictures in it. The finest paintings we saw in the country were two little gems of Murillo, in the private chamber of a resident gentleman, whose princely hospitality added one of the greatest charms to our visit. We unearthed also a museum of Aztec antiquities—pitched and piled helter-skelter in two or three mean rooms, with a carelessness reflecting great discredit upon the Mexican Government. Here is the miraculous banner once borne before the victorious Cortes; and few sweeter faces have I seen than the pictured Virgin upon it. Here also is the feather shield of the great Montezuma, and near them all sorts of curious old Aztec and Spanish weapons, any number of hideous Indian idols, quaint jars and vases, primitive musical instruments, etc., etc. One of the strangest relics of all was a sacrificial yoke of stone, which gives a very striking idea of what Aztec heathenism was—an impression intensified to the last degree when one has seen in the court below the immense sacrificial stone, round, weirdly sculptured and channelled for the victim's blood—when, with knives of flint, the heart was dug from the still living body, and cast at the idol's feet!

It were much to be desired that the Mexican people should devote a little of that superfluous energy, which they are ever expending in revolutions, and with which they sent such a respectable display to "the Centennial," toward the collection and formation of a worthy museum of antiquities.

There are few other public buildings of particular interest in the city. The college is a noble, spacious, substantial edifice, and apparently well-appointed. The collections of natural history are remarkably creditable to the country. There are also some good hospitals, of old foundation, one of them—that of "Jesus"—containing a veritable portrait of Cortes, and once having held his ashes. The place of their final deposit is not known.

One of the most interesting and attractive resorts in the capital is the old market-place, where you may see to-day the very people, costumes, habits and food, which the *Conquistadores* found and marvelled at more than three centuries ago—a chattering, chaffering, half-clad crowd of Indians, under booths, and with a variety of tropical vegetables and fruits, from which you obtain a good idea of the marvellous capabilities and advantages of the Mexican soil and climate. But as regards these fruits, we cannot but express our preference for a good peach or apple to all their luxuriant insipidity. And so it is with almost all things tropical; for character and strength you must go to the sterner, severer North—and thus we have much of the moral of history!

A word about the private residences in the city of Mexico. Many of them are of palatial proportions, and most inviting to the passer-by, with their courtyards and galleries and flowers. One of them, near our hotel, is most gorgeously tiled over its whole exterior, and several, indeed, would vie with any palaces in Europe. The Iturbide Hotel was the palace of that rash and unfortunate monarch, and is strikingly grand. The accommodations there, as elsewhere, are excellent, the restaurant separate from the lodging; and one can live in the best travelling style and comfort for two or three dollars a day in gold. With every convenience of living, and every fascination of interest, what can the tourist ask more or better than a visit to the city of Mexico?

VI.

THE ENVIRONS OF THE CITY OF MEXICO.

BUILDINGS NEAR THE SQUARE OF THE CATHEDRAL.

THE environs of the city of Mexico may be said to equal, if not to exceed in interest, the city itself. There is an almost monotonous regularity about the latter, much relieved, however, by the beautiful parks, the markets, and such delightful old squares as, *e. g.*, that of the Inquisition, where the flavor of the cruel yet creamy past becomes absolutely intense; where one finds all sorts of antique odds and ends exposed for sale under the arcades, and you enter the picturesque church and find idolatry to your heart's content, (we speak to those zealous souls who are so easily made happy by the detection of undueness in their neighbor's worship!). We must with sadness admit that what we witnessed in the dim old church of the Inquisition was very gross—grosser than anything we remember to have seen in the older world.

Life-size representations of the Saviour, seated, and revoltingly wounded, and also as dead from the Cross, met one in the nave; and all about the walls there was a profusion of the tawdriest decoration.

But enough of this, in all pity! Let us start out on this lovely Spring afternoon, (in February!) for a drive to Chapultepec, and pray do not be so intensely patriotic as to think at once of Gen. Scott and his yesterday victories over a half-caste and degenerate people; but lift your soul to the romantic level of Montezuma and his barbaric glory.

It is not a long drive—some four or five miles—but far enough to make it very unsafe at certain times. The avenues are very fine in every direction from the city, well-paved, and planted with trees, the newest and handsomest towards Chapultepec being called after the unhappy Empress Carlotta, to whom, as to her imperial husband, so many of the improvements in and about the city are due. But, we repeat, upon no one of them is it considered safe to drive after dark. The very boulevard which on Mardigras afternoon was thronged with vehicles, cavaliers, and populace, in the gayest and most festive appearance, (such a scene of costumes and characteristics as you must now go to Mexico to behold) at dusk becomes absolutely deserted — and woe to the unlucky and belated one!

Not long before our visit to the city, a wealthy proprietor was caught and carried off, and after a persistent search, his friends found him in a secluded hovel, buried up to his neck and gagged, while his inhuman captors were awaiting the exorbitant ransom.

Another instance: we were so fortunate as to breakfast at the princely villa in the pretty village of Tacubaya, near Chapultepec, of one of Mexico's most distinguished millionaires. The plate upon the hospitable board was worth a fortune; but when a little later we were looking into the dining-room, the domestics were hastily packing it up to be taken back to the city before night.

And this genial gentleman himself would scarcely dare to pass a night in his own elegant retreat — O, the *Sister Republic!*

Near the foot of the hill of Chapultepec stands an interesting relic of Montezuma's glory, in the shape of what is called his "swimming baths," in a most inviting spot, with large and deep tanks of cool, clear water, and with a surrounding structure recently decorated in Pompeian style. It is a favorite resort for the city people. A swarthy son of the Aztecs was induced, for a consideration, to disport himself in the pellucid depths for our amusement.

But the crowning glory of Chapultepec is found in its venerable and majestic trees, which are worthy to stand beside the cedars of Lebanon and the pines of Mariposa. They are of the cypress family, and many in number. It would be safe to say that some of them are forty or fifty feet in diameter. Their umbrageous summits tower into the blue summer sky, and it is easy to understand how Montezuma was accustomed to seek their restful shelter. The grounds wherein they stand surround extensively the castled hill, and even in their comparative neglect are most delightsome.

The palace of Chapultepec is now undergoing extensive repairs, and but little remains of its earlier character. Yet it is not without a thrill that one stands on foundations reared by a Montezuma, and gazes on a prospect that must often have rejoiced his eyes, as well as those of his conqueror Cortes, and of their strange successors, Maximilian and Juarez.

The view from the tower is unsurpassed—fair as the *Vega* of Granada, and in the season of moisture, doubtless as fascinating as the plain of Damascus. Almost at our feet lies the great city, beautifully embowered in its perennial green, and surrounded with its imperial avenues, its charming villages, and gleaming lakes, and towering above all in the glittering distance, the twin snow-crowned guardians of the majestic valley.

Another delightful excursion from the city is to "the floating gardens." We started early, to avoid the heat of the day, and took a covered boat in the canal, which leads to Lake Chalco. Near to our point of departure stands the striking monument to the last and one of the worthiest of the Aztec Emperors—Gautemozin—who did all that patriotism and valor could to save his already doomed and divided country. The canal is only about twenty-five feet wide, and very shallow, but is a thoroughfare for country produce. It was an animated and picturesque scene, as we were "poled" along, often through crowds of scows and canoes, laden to the water's edge with vegetables, firewood, grain, bags of sugar, etc., etc., and skilfully propelled by dusky Indians, very scantily clad, but cheerful and contented-looking—as who could fail to be beneath such a genial sun?

Soon we were gliding between low, verdant banks, bordered principally with willows, and at intervals passing little Indian villages of wigwams, surrounded with pleasant gardens and refreshing shade.

You turn from the main canal into smaller cuttings, just wide enough for your boat, and intersecting in every direction, and find yourself among the so-called "floating gardens." Formerly, as we read, a great deal of the watery environs of the city were thus occupied, and magical must have been the effect of these rich and variegated patches of *terra firma*, being moved from place to place, or anchored, and swaying gently to the ripples and the breeze. First formed by vegetable accumulations, and added to by careful art, they soon became, under the Aztecs, a leading means of industry and wealth. What remains of them to-day is mostly stationary, and irrigated by a sort of deep shovel, reminding one of the primitive Nile methods. These gardens are very brilliant and beautiful, rejoicing this day of early March in a profusion of vegetables, fruit and flowers.

About three miles from the capital we came to the old village of Sta. Anita, as primitive looking and picturesque a place as one could desire to visit. The Indian huts take you back to the *fellaheen* hovels of Egypt, though, we are glad to add, not as squalidly wretched. The more pretentious buildings have the same Spanish character as elsewhere.

THE ENVIRONS OF THE CITY OF MEXICO. 63

There is the same old *Fonda*, and the same sleepy, dilapidated public square—suggestive of everything but progress, and hence so refreshing to eyes fresh from "the States."

Hearing a loud, confused hum of voices, we entered a building on the square, and found a public school, though how they could learn anything under such Babel-like circumstances it was difficult to imagine. It sounded as if every one were reciting something different at once!

Just beyond was the village church, and entirely characteristic—an old, rude structure, with tawdry interior, and an odd-looking wooden representation of Cortes on horseback. In the yard we observed the singular custom of skulls and bones placed and piled above the graves or on the stones—a revolting sight, certainly indicating a low state of civilization and religion. The considerable number of disused and decaying chapels in the neighborhood was likewise a sad evidence of the latter: but what else can we expect from a country where the worst elements of Spanish ignorance, bigotry, and intolerance have taken root and thriven?

Surely with all our missions to the ends of the earth, we might find means and energies for conveying to this fair and favoring land some portion of those spiritual benefits and advantages, for which we have just been thanking our fathers' God in the hundredth year of our national existence.

VII.

THE ENVIRONS OF THE CITY OF MEXICO.
(Continued.)

"OUR LADY OF GUADALUPE."

WHAT Loretto is to Italy, Einsideln to Switzerland, the Atocha to Spain, and Lourdes just now to France, is Guadalupe to Mexico—the holy city of patriotic pilgrimage! Human nature demands such things, and will have them in some shape or other. Nations, like individuals, in times of need ask a sign from Heaven, and apotheosize their own interpretation. Only woe to the nation and woe to the Church, when the former, asking bread, receives from the latter a stone!

The Spanish conquerors of Mexico were not troubled with scruples. The conscience of their Church was as elastic then as it is to-day. Let me tell you the story of Guadalupe, premising that it is but a change of scene; the main elements have been the same in every age since Hildebrand.

The facts are taken from a sermon of a Cardinal of "the Holy Roman Church." The hero this time is—as might be expected—a converted Indian, who "on his way to study the Christian doctrine," passed by a mountain near to the city of Mexico. To him appeared the Blessed Virgin, and told him to seek the then Bishop, and to say to him in her name that she desired him to come and worship her on that very spot. On his return to the mountain the Virgin reappeared to receive his report. Our friend replied that he had not succeeded in obtaining an interview with the Bishop. "Return, and tell him that I, Mary, the mother of God, have sent you," was her answer.

The second time the Indian was admitted to the Episcopal presence, but his Right Reverence very naturally declined belief until he received some satisfactory evidence of the apparition. The patient Aztec returns to the holy spot with the message for "our Lady," who appears to him the third time.

THE ENVIRONS OF THE CITY OF MEXICO.

She simply commands him to ascend the mountain, and to "cut roses" for her.

Now Juan Diego knew perfectly well the mountain was entirely destitute of vegetation; but with exemplary faith he makes the attempt, *finds the flowers*, and brings them happily to the Virgin. She throws them in his *tilma*, (a part of his loose Indian dress,) and says, "Return once more to the Bishop, and tell him that these flowers are the credentials of your mission." The honored native departs, and admitted to the Bishop's presence, unfolds his robe to present the roses, "when lo! there appeared on the rude garment that blessed picture of the Virgin, which now, after three centuries, still exists, without having suffered the slightest injury!" The Virgin once more appears to our favored friend, the Indian, restores his uncle to health, and tells him "the image on thy *tilma* I wish called the Virgin of Guadalupe!"

The image itself passed from the oratory of the Bishop to the shrine of the great collegiate Church—one of the wealthiest in the world. You will find a copy of the picture, as a household god, literally speaking, in every orthodox Mexican home. The name of "Maria de Guadalupe" designates a large proportion of Mexico's fair daughters. She is, indeed, the Patron Saint of Mexico, in accordance with the proud motto beneath, "Non fecit taliter omni nationi!"

So much for the fanciful legend, and now for an excursion to the shrine itself. It is only two or three miles from the capital, and is reached by frequent and rapid horse cars. And what is better, you may, by paying a little more, travel in first-class and very neat carriages, with plenty of room—a refinement of civilization which we unprejudiced Americans have not yet reached.

It is a very pleasant road, one of the old Aztec avenues, refreshingly bordered with tropical green; but the village of Guadalupe, which is the terminus, is decidedly unprepossessing—very religiously mean and dirty! The church itself is not large, but barbarously rich within. There is the same peculiar arrangement of choir and altar as in the Cathedral of Mexico. Above the altar, gorgeously encased in precious metals and gems, is the poor Indian's pictured *tilma*—the wonder-working Madonna of Guadalupe. The long, large rail-work of choir, altar, aisle, etc., is all of silver, as are also candelabra, lecterns, etc., etc.—such an overwhelming effect of wealth as we believe to be unique.

There is nothing in Europe more exquisite than the choir wood-carvings. They are in high relief, of scenes from the life of our Lord—every one a study of delight. There are, of course, a number of pictures, but few of much merit. Among the worst are the native attempts to represent the miraculous story; and, as is universally the case, the most unfortunate are the *ex voto* offerings and efforts of art, and yet each one of them, as we must reverently remember, representing a world of tragic reality and faithful sentiment.

Everywhere, indeed, within the consecrated interior, is a blaze of gold and silver, rich gems and marbles, while just without, at the very door, lies the usual assortment of crouching, crippled beggary; and to crown the whole, in the porch of this most sacred and suggestive shrine, you are invited to purchase a lottery ticket!

Passing from the church up a winding street, you come shortly to the miraculous well, its waters having been blessed by the Virgin to the cure of all manner of fleshly ills. It is protected by a small chapel, which is constantly thronged with the faithful. We found the water disagreeable to the taste, which however may indicate the presence of some effective mineral agent.

From this chapel a steep, stone stairway ascends to the summit of the hill, where stands another and smaller church, marking the actual site of the miraculous gift. This temple is devoid of any æsthetic interest; but from the pavement in front is a charming view of plain and mountain, lake and city, certainly none the less refreshing as you turn from the sad desecration of faith around you.

And as we rode homeward, in the cool, quiet eventide, we could not but reflect again upon the unchanging and unchangeable aspects of human nature, which enwrap the fabled mount of Guadalupe with the same fatal gloom overshadowing the seven hills of fallen Rome!

VIII.

THE ENVIRONS OF THE CITY OF MEXICO.

(Continued.)

THE PYRAMIDS OF SAN JUAN TEOTIHUACAN.

"The City of the gods."

OF all the excursions in the Mexican valley, that to the pyramids of San Juan Teotihuacan is by far the most interesting to the student of the past. There hangs about them a mystery not even possessed by the much greater antiquity of the Egyptian monuments. Scholars have examined, excavated, studied and searched, but cannot well decide as to which of those great tribes and nations, that swept down successively from the sterner North to occupy these rich table-lands, the origin of these pyramids is due; and yet, if we assign them, as is common, to the Toltec race, we cannot go further back than the sixth century of our era. It is a mystery almost unparalleled in the annals of history. There they stand, and not alone, for similar erections are found at Cholula and elsewhere, pyramids reaching even to the grandeur of Egypt's, of which we now have entirely satisfactory explanations— monuments of a regal past, which has churlishly left us no sign nor story—a mystery like that of the vast mounds and massive ruins found in our own far West, which we believe the best studies would assign, as a prior construction, to the same lost and buried people.

It is more than idle to doubt their artificial character. They bear every evidence of careful labor in form, material, color, arrangement, relics, etc., as we shall proceed to show. Indeed we may now say that our own unprejudiced examination convinced us of the probable truth of the generally received theory on the subject, that these pyramids of San Juan Teotihuacan, with their many neighboring mounds, were erected with immediate reference to sacrificial and sepulchral purposes.

"But you certainly will not visit them in this unsettled state of the country—a revolution going on, with rebel raids, and even rebel watch-fires pointed out on the distant hill-sides. You must not think of it. It is not safe—" etc. etc., were the kind and encouraging remarks of American and Mexican friends alike. We were a trifle staggered at first, but an experience of similar warnings in southern Italy, Sicily, Spain, and the East, had long since convinced us that if you want to do or see a thing very much, you had better try it, unless you are personally and absolutely sure of harm; and then, if it is only the matter of a few dollars' loss, why, put them in your pocket before you start, that your brigand brethren may not be induced to harshness by their disappointment. "Never turn back on a mere rumor or report," ought to be a maxim graven on the back or at the head of every guide-book. We have known friends to lose the best things of all foreign travel by what we cannot but consider an over-prudence in such matters; and we ourselves have been more than once rewarded by the infinite satisfaction, almost equal to that of the actual visit, of not having allowed ourselves to be stopped by idle, fear-begotten tales.

So behold us, very early on a fresh Spring morning, in the train for San Juan—very early, indeed, for we were well on our way before "old Sol" condescended to rise and beam rubicundly on the sleeping snows of Popocatepetl. It was glorious to see her, and her fair sister Istacyhuatl flush with queenly joy at his return, and open a way for his kingly light over their trackless slopes to the sweet smiling plains below.

San Juan is a few stations from Mexico on the way to Vera Cruz. We were there by 7 A. M., and found at the little station, what is to be found, indeed, everywhere, as we believe to have before remarked, an excellent cup of coffee, good bread, and a civil stationmaster, not omitting to mention a more than willing Indian to guide us. This Indian was not alone, it is unnecessary to remark. His friends and neighbors were with him on speculative errand. These natives were of all ages, and all equally anxious to dispose of the many little image relics, which, we incline to think, are as yet too abundantly found, and the place, moreover, too little visited, to require manufacture. Doubtless when the supply is exhausted, and "Brown, Jones, and Robinson" have finally reached here, under the fatherly guidance of Mr. Cook, we will see that the genius of this aspiring age, which has sent *scarabei* to Egypt, "antiques" to Italy, and idols to Africa, will not be wanting to the Mexican emergency.

Where these Indians all lived was at first a mystery, for which indeed we were prepared on such an expedition. Nothing in the way of buildings was visible but the station, and an independent looking old church near by; but we soon discovered a collection of hovels almost concealed by hedges of gigantic cacti. We had never seen such immense plants of the kind—frequently so large that we could sit in their shade, and constituting with the pepper tree the principal vegetation of the fields and mounds.

The pyramids are several miles distant from the hamlet, and to tell the whole warning truth, the way is through ploughed fields and under a burning sun. But we doubt that the eagerness of the gold or diamond seeker is greater, and certainly it is not as wholesome, as that with which we explored the furrows for pottery relics, and to our frequent success. The peasants, in their rude, primitive ploughing, turn up quantities of these little heads, and most remarkable to relate, we found no two alike. They are almost all extremely grotesque; sometimes with crowns or other emblematic covering. Occasionally they possess a neck; some even rejoice in shoulders, and may vie with the conventional cherub; but few, very few indeed, are ever found of a complete figure. For some mysterious reason the Aztec artificer could only reproduce the master part of the human frame; and when we accept the theory that these countless fragilities were given by the Aztec priests connected with these sacrificial pyramids, as idols or image souvenirs to the myriads of pilgrim worshippers, we can perhaps better conjecture about the secret of their form. And not only do you pick up these curious heads, but also a double-socket piece of pottery, apparently intended for purposes of light, and greatest rarity of all, we found in a furrow, a small rude calendar, also of pottery, and circular, with singular hieroglyphics.

The first pyramid we ascended was that called the Pyramid of the Sun. Its base line measures over seven hundred feet, and its perpendicular height is more than two hundred feet, (we find that measurements differ.) The ascent is arduous—a broiling sun would suffice to make it so; but when is added a surface of sharp lava stones, one is forcibly reminded of Vesuvius-climbing. There are frequent traces of a former coating of cement, and very marked signs of terracing. The interior, as far as excavated, seems to be of layers of stones, tufa, mud, etc. The summit area is level, and measures about sixty feet by ninety, with an almost perfect orientation.

Clavigero states that there were formerly temples on these pyramids, and within them immense idols of stone, covered with gold. The Pyramid of the Sun had in its grooved breast a large golden image of the planet, which was soon added to the treasures of the Spanish conquerors, and the idol was overthrown by the orders of the Bishop—some of the huge fragments in the neighborhood probably formed a part of it.

There can be little doubt that these ancient structures were models of the later Aztec Teocallis—those curious temple mounds, which were the centre of worship in all Aztec communities. It is conjectured that their ruinous, and now almost natural surface of earth and vegetation is due to the effort made by the more civilized founders to cover and conceal them from future savage invasions. And, at the risk of repetition, we must add that their remarkable correspondence to similar Egyptian constructions adds, if anything, to the piquancy of mystery enveloping them.

We found the summit strewn with various *débris*, and among them many evidently wrought pieces of obsidian, which was the flinty material of the knives used in Aztec sacrifice.

The view from this elevation is very striking, not only of the surrounding country with its grand features and peculiar vegetation, but also of the many mounds or *tumuli*, arranged with more or less of regularity in groups and squares, and most remarkably in one long avenue extending between the two great pyramids. If, from the vast amount of ruinous remains by the river-bed and elsewhere near, antiquarian conjecture be true that a mighty city once occupied their site, have we not here a wonderful sacrificial and sepulchral suburb, like unto those of Egypt, Greece, and Rome in their proudest days?

What has been said of the Sun Pyramid will apply

to the Pyramid of the Moon, except that the latter is smaller, and that within it have been discovered some passages and chambers, but nothing to indicate their character.

The avenue of *tumuli* between, called by native tradition "the path of the dead," is one of the most interesting and mysterious features of the whole arrangement. These mounds reach to thirty feet in height, and are entirely overgrown with vegetation, though in some of them are remains of masonry and stucco, and even of color. The avenue is two hundred and fifty feet wide, and we found the well-preserved remains of terrace steps descending from the mounds to the roadway.

Much of the solid material used in their construction, as also of the idol statues, has been destroyed or carried away from that same vandal instinct which is robbing everywhere the monumental past; or, at the best, transferring to museums that which only has its proper value amid the associations of its history. But still we found, as before remarked, some massive fragments, and especially one immense monolithic idol, almost perfect in preservation, standing in a helpless, half-disinterred condition, most wonderfully suggestive, may we add, of that poor Pagan past, which an aping materialism would seek presently to revive.

Besides these pyramids and mounds there are other curious formations, one called the "Citadel," a large and regularly embanked square, and also several smaller enclosures, the natural floor of which was as level and smooth as though it had been rolled but yesterday. It is probable that a huge idol stood on a central mound of these sepulchral squares.

Altogether, the quantity and vastness of these remains, and the doubt concerning them—their purposes and history, makes San Juan Teotihuacan one of the most interesting of modern problems, and most delightful of excursions. As we returned to the capital in the early evening, fatigued indeed from the heat and effort, but laden with Indian relics, and safe as regards our skins and ducats, we could not but feel that here again was much more than enough to repay a trip to Mexico.

TERRA COTTA HEAD.
Found near the Pyramids of San Juan Teotihuacan.

IX.

THE CITY OF MEXICO AND ITS ENVIRONS.
(Concluded.)

ONE of the most interesting excursions in the neighborhood of the Capital is to the famous old tree of the *Noche Trista*. The story is, that during the terrible retreat of Cortes from the city, when his little veteran army was beset by myriads of outraged and relentless foes, until the very canals ran blood, and the broken bridges were replaced by piles of dead and dying warriors, the great captain rallied and rested his shattered and dispirited forces near this enormous tree, making it his own shelter, if we remember rightly the tradition. It is situated about a couple of miles from the city, and reached by convenient horse-cars, on a beautiful and shaded avenue. On the way you pass that saddest and most suggestive spot in every foreign city—the Protestant cemetery. Nothing could be more retired and delightfully laid out than this last resting-place for wanderers in restless Mexico.

We found the historical tree to be of the same family as the Chapultepec giants, and of almost equal proportions, but sadly decayed, and apparently much mutilated by fuel and relic hunters; now protected, however, by a substantial railing.

Could such trees to their actual and patriarchal life only add the gift of speech, what tales could they not tell? Who would not more than delight to listen to the mystic and majestic eloquence of Lebanon's lofty cedars, or better still, to thrill beneath the whisper of Gethsemane's sacred olives? So this old tree of the *Noche Trista* could doubtless reveal such a scene of bitter tears and utter agony as hardly to be believed, in that bood-stained drama of ruthless greed, called "the Conquest of Mexico."

And, speaking of military achievements leads us to the relation of a brief interview we had with the once famous Santa Anna, whose decease we have noticed in the public journals since our return home. The old man was then very infirm, being in his eightieth year, and requiring support as he stood. He received us in his plain dwelling with exceeding courtesy, as gallant to the ladies of our party as though he were welcoming them from the heyday of his dictatorial throne. It was not very difficult to read in the wreck of that strong countenance and vigorous frame the secret of a turbulent and vicissitudinous career—a career that might have led to anything and everything, perhaps, had it been based on the incorruptibility of a Juarez, had it combined with native force the magnanimity of a Maximilian.

There is, indeed, no doubt about the brains of Mexico. With such men, as she possesses, at her helm, she may hope for any grandeur of the future. Faith, honesty, patience are her special need of the present; and may we always do our political part and fraternal duty as well, in sending to represent us at "our sister republic," such high-toned Christian gentlemen as he who now honors us by his diplomatic service—it is with pleasure and gratitude we mention his name—Mr. Foster, of Indiana.

And so we must say good-bye to the grand old city! We feel we have not half done it justice.

There is so much of pleasing and varied interest coming up in every street, at every corner. The light, the air, the costumes and characteristics form a continual feast of luxuriant and stimulating beauty. We wished much to visit the silver mines of the interior, and the fair city of Cuernavaca, once the princely home of Cortes. We were even tempted to try a passage across the country to the Pacific coast — Acapulco or Manzanilla; but lack of time, wretched accommodations for ladies, and last but not least, the increasing revolution, made it seem the sheerest folly, as was indeed proven by the unsuccessful attempt of a more daring friend.

The military condition of the atmosphere became really exciting before we left the capital. The streets were full of soldiers, and everything looked as if the nervousness of our good Mexican friends had attained some foundation of fact. We found the guards doubled on all the trains, which did not in the least, however, diminish our enjoyment of the ride to Puebla. We returned by the railway to Vera Cruz as far as Apizaco, which is four or five hours from the city of Mexico; and here occurred an incident, which, fortunately, we can relate with entire equanimity, and which will give the uninitiated a good idea of how some matters are managed in a southern republic.

Thanks to the exceeding courtesy of the managing director of the road, a special car was placed at our disposition, and a special servant was assigned to take charge of it. At Apizaco we breakfasted very comfortably, and started off on the branch line to Puebla. One of our party, taking up his wallet soon after, discovered that the lock had been tampered with, and a roll of silver dollars extracted. The writer of this was not long in examining his own bag, and found himself the only other tourist thus distinguished.

What is now to be done? Of course the silver is lost, but there is some satisfaction in complaint, and most happily a station where we can telegraph is close at hand—only about an hour from Puebla, (mark this fact!) Hardly have we stopped before one of our friends—ever kindly, cool, and considerate—has jumped out and sent a despatch back to Apizaco. We sink back in our seats, sigh again over our vanished dollars, and only wish they had gone to one of the many good works of the Reforming Church in the Capital—to the excellent orphanage, *e. g.*, or anywhere rather than to the rascal who got them!

"An hour passed on." We whistle up to the platform of Puebla. As we alight a uniformed official approaches and courteously begs the gentleman who has telegraphed to step to the office of the superintendent.

Visions of legal difficulties and detentions float across our anxious minds. We enter the little room, and find another gentlemanly agent, who with scarcely any preliminaries, inquires the amount we have lost, and to our exact reply hands us back all our dear, lost dollars, save one. Surely this is "presto magic!" And how could it all so quickly have been accomplished? It seems our dispatch had aroused the whole responsible force at Apizaco. Mutual conference failed to disclose any suspicion of the employés there; but distrust was expressed respecting the special servant of our car, and orders were immediately telegraphed to Puebla to have him arrested on the arrival of our train. This was promptly done. The money was found on him, and he was lodged in jail before we reached our own hotel! No deposition, no trial, no inconvenience to any one but the criminal, who was sent on to the army the next day, his punishment being to fight the battles of his country! " *Dulce est*," etc.

For promptitude, precision, and entire absence of unnecessary formalities, we challenge the nineteenth century to produce anything more satisfactory!

VIEW IN THE PLAZA IN THE CITY OF PUEBLA.

X.

PUEBLA AND CHOLULA.

THE city of Puebla ranks next to the Capital in size and importance, and first in religious estimation. It lies at about the same elevation as the City of Mexico, with picturesque environs, culminating on the one side in solitary and sombre Malinche—a name of interest from its having been applied by the natives to both Cortes and his fair and faithful Indian companion—and on the other side, in our old volcanic friends Popocatepetl and Istacyhuatl. You will remember that the march of the Spanish conquerors, after the occupation and massacre of Cholula, was over the lofty ridge connecting the two great mountains, whence first dawned upon their wayworn vision the bewildering fascinations of the valley of Mexico.

Puebla is well-built, well-preserved, clean, and

contains about seventy thousand inhabitants; but to the enlightened American, all these advantages will be almost annulled by the fact that it has not one daily newspaper!

Our hotel was ideal. Fancy a picturesque old convent, toned by age into all softness of color and shade, built around a court half-filled with old-fashioned coaches—fancy stepping from your balconied room out into a glorious cloister, where bordered and bloomed tropical flowers and warbled an aviary of tropical birds!

Fancy this by a Mexican sunlight; fancy it by a Mexican moonlight, and you have the Hotel des Diligences in Puebla. And when we add that the beds are good and the table fair, you will see that a few days in Puebla are not at all to be dreaded.

Though threatened by revolution without and within, yet the town seemed quiet and orderly, and we soon set forth to become better acquainted with it. We found many nice-looking shops, and a number of attractive churches. The Cathedral stands on one side of the grand square, which is handsomely laid out, and surrounded on the other sides with business arcades.

In considering this Cathedral, we are brought to explain our allusion above to the sacred primacy of the Pueblan city. It is honored by the name of "Puebla de los Angeles," because in the building of its great church, these holy co-workers were said to have done as much by night as the people did by day. Each morning's light displayed the miraculous addition!

Though smaller than the Cathedral of Mexico, it is more magnificent in almost every respect. It may readily be called one of the finest churches in the world. It is of basaltic material, supported by massive buttresses, and surmounted by lofty towers.

As is usual in Latin countries, it stands on an immense platform, reached by steps at several points, and adding much to the grandness of effect.

Its interior arrangement is similar to that of the Cathedral of Mexico, with its mass of altars and choir taking up the middle of the nave, and sadly modifying the impression. But its gorgeous decorations— of gilding everywhere—over altars and baldacchino, columns and walls, its splendid paintings and carvings and marbles—all this makes a *tout ensemble* of bewildering majesty and beauty. The inlaid woodwork of the choir cannot be surpassed in all Europe. The old missals would honor any shelf of the Vatican, and beneath the grand altar is a vault chamber of precious marbles and metals for the interment of Puebla's bishops. No princely pope could prepare for himself a prouder sepulchre.

The sacristy is a gem of interest. Masterly paintings and most sumptuous appointments give it a regal air; and again we were struck by the magnificence of a marble lavatory. Italy can produce nothing to compare with it in our memory.

But perhaps the unique wonder of all is the chapter-room — an oblong, lofty apartment, hung with tapestries, which were presented to the Cathedral by Charles V., having been worked by the ladies of his court. The subjects are mostly allegorical, concerning the newly discovered and conquered Americas.

There hang also on the walls most interesting portraits of the great Emperor and of the Pueblan

Bishops. The old furniture of the room would make an antiquary's mouth fairly to water.

The view from the belfry is superb. The city lies mapped out before you, and you read much of the history of this most romantic country in the surrounding beauty and grandeur of configuration.

Our native guide, however, as well as several irrepressible youths, who had followed him, took much more interest in pointing out to us the scenes of recent revolutionary conflict, an engagement with the "Pronunciamentos" having taken place only the day before.

Indeed our evening was mostly spent in discussing our own relations to the exciting state of affairs, our chances of further sight-seeing, and of escape to the sea coast. An ultimatum had been sent to the railway company by the rebels, with the threat that if the amount of money demanded were not forthcoming, the road would be cut. It was understood that the allotted period had about expired, and that the Company had refused the outrageous demand. The prospect of a compulsory sojourn in Puebla, under the circumstances, was not altogether one of charms! But we could not give up Cholula, and —thanks very much to the kind encouragement and assistance of a resident American missionary—we were not obliged to do so. Not but that we received warnings enough on all hands, and were considered, indeed, as running our heads unnecessarily into the lion's mouth.

We called on a government official, who said he would give us an escort, if possible; but when the hour of departure arrived, no soldiers had appeared, and so our little party set out, as true tourists should ever do, "sans peur et sans reproche."

Cholula is about three leagues distant from Puebla. The road is tolerable, and we found comfortable and cheap conveyances. It was a very quiet drive; the engagement of a day or two previous would account for the absence of vehicles, but allow for the frequent passing of poor, pedestrian peasants — principally women—wearily returning from market, and occasionally an armed and savage-looking horseman, whose weapons, however, were probably only for self-defence in this Ishmaelitish country.

The land looked fertile, and was green with

promising crops, especially as we approached Cholula, which must have been a garden spot of loveliness and wealth.

The world-famed Pyramid rises conspicuously out of the plain, but appearing less definitely marked as you approach it. In fact, as compared with that of San Juan, it is a disappointment—its pyramidal character being almost destroyed by the ravages of time. Its edges are very much broken, and its sides are entirely overgrown. But it is of much easier ascent. Indeed you could drive to the summit over a broad road constructed by the Spaniards, and leading to the commanding Church, dedicated to the Virgin of Remedios. This chapel was a substitution by the Spaniards for the worship of Quetzalcoatl, the great, good and fair god of the Aztecs. Having been destroyed, (by fire, we believe,) the church has been recently reconstructed, and decorated with that cheap tawdriness of taste, which, we regret to say, has become characteristic of Roman Church interiors.

The central object of worship upon the grand altar is one of those doll-images, in which the invincible conquerors placed such credulous reliance.

The original image of the celebrated Virgin de los Remedios is said to have been carried to Mexico by a soldier of Cortes' army. After the terrible Noche Trista, it was concealed, and indeed, altogether disappeared for a time; it was reserved for a lucky Indian to discover it in a maguey plant on the summit of a barren mountain. It was a day of jubilee for the Spaniards. A church was built on the spot, which soon became a frequented shrine, with attendant priests, treasurer, camarista, etc., etc. She became the rich object of endowments, votive offerings, legacies, etc., was carried about in time of drought, and adored by the passers by, the Viceroy himself leading her train. She became the great rival of our Indian Lady of Guadalupe. On one occasion of victory she was brought to the City of Mexico dressed as a general; on another of defeat, her passport was signed to leave the country, which sentence was not, however, carried out. Well may we pray—'God save such a State!'

From the tower of this church you have a most

comprehensive and satisfactory view, as also, we should remark, from the extensive summit area on which the church is built. The effect of looking over the parapet wall upon the artificially precipitous sides to the rich level plain below, is very striking.

The vast site of the ancient city is perfectly evident from the marked lines of its regular streets, stretching far beyond the now insignificant town into its surrounding fields and plantations. From this observation we should judge the pyramid or Teocalli to have occupied the centre of the old Cholula, which was in its glory before the tenth century of our era. But tradition would seem to indicate that this pyramid was built even earlier, probably as early as the sixth or seventh century—the Olmec period of Mexican history.

Its base—about 1440 feet square, and covering forty acres—is thus more than twice as large as Cheops. The Mexican pyramid is about two hundred feet high, which is a little more than the elevation of Egyptian Mycerinus. Its summit platform is about two hundred feet square. Its sides face the cardinal points, and show marked traces of four terraced stories. It seems to have been built of adobe, with alternate layers of clay or rubble.

Humboldt's remarks respecting it are most interesting. "The construction of the teocalli recalls the oldest monuments to which the history of our race reaches." . . . "Imagine a square four times greater than that of the Place Vendome in Paris, covered with layers of bricks, rising to twice the elevation of the Louvre!"

As regards the object and use of this great monument, it is but a repetition of the wonder and mystery of San Juan. No thorough excavation or examination has ever been made of the interior.

A tomb chamber has been found, which contained two skeletons, some idols and pottery; but from the relative position and character of this tomb, it can hardly be supposed that sepulture was the main, original object of the pyramid.

Within known times there has always been a temple of worship upon the summit. Frequently destroyed by internecine wars, the magnificent structure suffered its final demolition by the invading Spaniards—to be replaced by idol worship in another form!

A MEXICAN IDOL.

XI.

CHOLULA—*Continued.*

"Mexitli, woman-born, who, from the womb,
  Child of no mortal sire, leap'd terrible,
The armed avenger of his mother's fame;
And he whose will the subject winds obey,
Quetzalcoatl; and Tlaloc, water-god,
And all the hosts of deities, whose power
Requites with bounty Aztlan's pious zeal,
Health and rich increase giving to her sons,
And withering in the war her enemies."

Southey's Madoc.

OUR brief study of the pyramid of Cholula would lead us very appropriately to consider for a moment the subject of Mexican mythology, which, essentially linked as it is with Mexican history, must form a prime element of interest to the intelligent traveller.

All national and tribal histories begin with myths, out of whose mistiness tower grand deified forms and fancies of vice and virtue. Such are the histories of

Egypt, Greece and Rome—and such no less is the history of Anahuac.

There, as elsewhere, may we find to our Christian comfort, that the great central object of faith and adoration is a good and omnipotent GOD, whose worship—however perverted and corrupted—shows distinct traces of earliest and purest revelation.

It is this very perversion and corruption, which so soon makes other and meaner gods, and peoples the wilds of nature with creations of fear and favor.

Such was the terrible Huitzilopochtli—"the Mexican Mars"—a sanguinary monster, his shrine ever reeking with human sacrifices. And such, in lesser and varied degree, were many others—even to the least of all—"the Penates or household gods," whose images—according to a superstitious custom far from extinct even in Christian lands—were found in every dwelling.

Indeed, according to Prescott, who, with a historian's license, may possibly have exaggerated a little, it is more than astonishing to notice the ritual resemblances between the heathenism of the Aztecs and the religion introduced by the "most Catholic" conquerors—a resemblance extending even into the realm of sacraments.

It is a more than curious fact, that the symbol of the cross was known to the Indians before the arrival of Cortes. It is stated that a stone cross was found in Yucatan, and that a native prophet proclaimed the near arrival of a stranger race, bearing the cross as their symbol.

More wonderful still, in this very city of Cholula there is said to have been a temple of the Holy Cross in the Toltec era.

In Oajaca there was a cross regarded by the natives with the utmost veneration. By order of an early Spanish Bishop, it was sumptuously enshrined. An account of it, with a portion of its wood, in cross shape, was sent to Paul V., who welcomed it on his knees, to the hymn, "Vexilla Regis," etc.

How far all these statements and stories found root in the fertile and fashioning faith of the early Mexican Church, we will not attempt to determine. It is no more unlikely, however, that the simple, but sublime symbol should have been found amid the relics of the mysterious Mexican races, than that it should be seen to-day indelibly graven on the stone of Egypt's earliest temples.

But to return to our more immediate theme. By far the most interesting personage in Aztec mythology was he, whom we have previously mentioned — Quetzalcoatl — the grand, mysterious god of the earth and air—a character of real grace and glory—invested with an ideality and sublimity, to which it would be difficult to find an equal in the polluted Pantheon of Greece and Rome.

The traditions of Anahuac speak of an early inundation or "Deluge," from which escaped seven giants—one of whom went to Cholula and built a memorial hill in the shape of a pyramid. The gods were wrathful at this presumptuous attempt to reach the clouds of their habitation, and hurled fire from heaven, which destroyed and dispersed the workmen, and the work ceased. It is unnecessary to point the resemblance of this tradition to the narrative of Genesis.

This monument was afterwards dedicated to Quetzalcoatl. He was the benefactor—the Saturn—of the early Mexicans. He was noble of figure, wise and pure of character. He introduced law and order. He promoted industry and art. In his reign agriculture flourished, and wealth prevailed. "The corn grew so strong that a single ear was a load for a man." Luscious fruits perfumed the air and satisfied the sense, and countless birds of song and beauty charmed the soul.

It was a time too fair to last. The gods were jealous, perhaps. They desired to drive him from Tula, where sat his throne. He was offered a beverage of immortality, which he readily drank—(as who would not?) He was then tempted to wander vaguely away from his kingdom. He came to Cholula, where they compelled him to become their king, and where he sustained his lofty character of wisdom, justice and humanity.

But the spell was upon him; his fair, visionary kingdom of Tlapalla beckoned him ever on. At last he arrives at the borders of the bright, mysterious sea. He dismisses his noble and virtuous attendants, bidding them to comfort his subject Cholulans, and to assure them of his happy and hopeful return. And so he disappears from human view—like our own Indian Hiawatha—vanishing into the dimness of the undiscovered waters, or better still, shall we not reverently say, like unto some Son of Man and God, who hath ascended from the race He hath taught and redeemed, that He may return one day to comfort and compensate all righteousness! For the Cholulans were disconsolate over Quetzalcoatl's departure. They made him their tutelary god, and this great pyramid we have just visited—crowned with a majestic temple—became the principal seat of his worship. He was "the god of the air." His symbol was a feathered serpent, with what particular reference is not known. His festivals became the great days of Mexico, his priesthood those of greatest influence. Their austerities were remarkable. "Every fourth or divine year these festivals were preceded by a rigid fast of eighty days!"

And the Mexicans never gave up looking for his blessed return. Its hope filled the faith and heart of their religion. When Cortes and his invincible band of adventurers landed on their coast, and the story flew on fleetest wings to the grand capital that the fair-haired and mighty strangers had arrived, speaking an unknown tongue, using unknown weapons, mounting on unknown beasts, leaving behind them in the obedient waters unknown and bird-like vessels, it brought a thrill of mingled and mysterious emotion to every heart in faithful and favored Anahuac—from the rude fisher on Tezcoco to the magnificent Montezuma on his throne.

And it was only when the sordid, grasping, cruel prowess of the Spaniards had overturned all hope and hospitality before it, and utterly precluded the possibility of peacefully winning these far from unsusceptible peoples to the gentle and genial religion of the Christ, that we see these mixed emotions all turned into bitterest—nay, let us call it patriotic hate—yet not before they had undermined the courage of the Aztec King, and prepared the way for the divided councils and desperate decisions, which themselves sealed the doom of the mightiest heathen empire the American continent has known!

Reluctantly leaving this fascinating subject, so intimately connected with the grand monument we have been studying, let us now descend to see what else of interest the modern Cholula presents to the tourist traveller.

Near the base of the Pyramid we entered a rude shop to ask for a drink of water, and were surprised to find behind the counter a woman of the people—a full-blooded Indian—presenting one of the most perfect types of beauty it was ever our pleasure to behold. The natives are usually too toil-worn to be fine-looking; the men appear strong, patient, and docile, the women seem to fade early beneath the exhausting influences of climate and care; but here was a young creature of a loveliness that any land would be proud to possess, and a Raphael would be privileged to paint. The curious old Aztec vase, purchased from her graceful poverty, and now upon a book-case in my study, remains a souvenir of admiring homage to God's fairest handiwork.

On one side of the large public square of the dilapidated old town stands one of the most remarkable churches in the whole country. We have not met with any written description of it, but so far as we could learn, it was built by Cortes, and would seem to have been suggested to him or to his companions by the Mosque Cathedral of Cordova.

The exterior effect is very striking, with its many small domes, and heavy blank walls, to which the appearance of a fortress is added by medieval battlements, as also by the bare surrounding and strongly walled enclosure. The church, by rough measurement, is about one hundred and fifty feet square, with comparatively low ceiling, which is relieved by forty-nine small domes, decorated with such singular devices as eyes, crescents, etc., etc. This interior is broken up by nearly fifty short columns. At one side is a platform chancel, and the high altar. There are a few small side-chapels, a rare old font and pulpit, and some interesting odds and ends of church furniture—the whole forming an ecclesiastical relic and picture of the past altogether unique, that cannot be matched, we venture to say, in all America.

The sad feature of the scene, was the apparent desertion and neglect of what, to our thinking, should form one of the proudest historical monuments in Mexico.

Our examination of this church completed what was of special interest in Cholula, though the faithful Cholulans themselves seemed to be having a good time that day, in the observance of one of the innumerable Church Festas—principally expressed to our ears by the discharge of artillery, but much more detrimental to the peace of mind of sundry faithless curs, who at each salvo beat an absurdly precipitate retreat.

As we drove home in the declining day, and saw the gorgeous sunset investing majestic Popocatepetl, and more gently lingering on the white brow of nearer Malinche, and then the crescent moon emerging to lend her slender, silver radiance to the eternal snows, with a gleam of mystic sentiment far down into the ever verdant valleys—we could not but feel that our day of tourist explorations had been only piquant in its peril and perfect in its satisfaction.

XII.

HOW WE TRIED TO GET TO XALAPA.

EARLY the next morning we bade a fond adieu to dear old "Puebla of the Angels," and succeeded without mishap in getting past the threatened junction of Apizaco; and not long after, were gliding down the grand sinuosities and sublime defiles of the great mountain railway. I think we enjoyed even more the descent, for the reason of greater facility in observation. Surely nothing could be finer than those views into the infinite tropical distance, and all the more striking, indeed, from the wonderful transitions, one moment rushing through a dark and devious defile, then bursting out into a vision of Paradise—sweet, smiling plains, time-hued old towers, and everywhere—on city, mount and valley, the exquisite play of light and shade, a very dream of beauty—to be awakened the next moment by a cautious creeping over some tremendous, thrilling iron span, making you suddenly to realize that after all, the path to that earthly paradise might easily become a "facilis descensus Averni!"

Then came the burning glory of the Tierra Caliente—glowing with ever summer heat, and only a little relieved as we neared Vera Cruz by one of the weirdest thunder storms we had ever witnessed. The sheet-lightning fairly lit up the darkly-laden heavens and sympathizing earth into a broad and burnished vividness that seemed as if it might have been from the charging cohorts of Heaven.

The heat was intense in Vera Cruz. We had several days to wait for our steamer. In fact, the threatening aspect of political affairs had led us to hasten somewhat to the coast, or at least to get away from the great central railway, which in all revolutions is likely to be the main point of attack.

We had heard so much of Xalapa—an old city about eighty miles in the mountainous interior from Vera Cruz—of its internal interest, its peerless environs—so fair and fertile, that some thirty or forty years ago, it is said, an English traveller arrived there to pass a night, and became so fascinated that he never left it afterwards. We had heard so much of all this, and the weather was so abominably hot, and our old friend, the French landlady, still so villanous, that we would not even take a full night's rest by the sea, but at a fearfully early hour of the following day, were up and off again—and, let it be recorded to our credit, all as amiable as ever!

We retraced our way by steam for about fifteen miles, and then began one of the oddest modes of travel it has been our fortune to try. Have you ever heard of a mule-way, or rather of a mule railway? The only full opportunity of enjoying one is, we believe, between Vera Cruz and Xalapa. The track is laid the whole distance, and the ultimate purpose is to employ steam throughout; but meanwhile a sturdy team of mules do the business with entire satisfaction—*i. e.*, if you have no objection to passing most of a day in one of the loveliest countries GOD ever made.

Thanks to the never-failing courtesy of the Railway Company, a special car—brand-new and open all around, thus affording a perfect view of everything—was placed at our disposal; the manager of the road—a young and genial American—was detailed to escort us, and soon we were rolling smoothly along behind six mules at full run, which were changed at intervals; and so we had old-fashioned post-chaising, with all the modern improvements.

Words would fail to tell the glory of nature through which we were passing. We had already seen much of it, but at a distance, whirled through it by impatient steam; now we were brought face to face—aye, hand to hand with *Madra Natura* in all her wealth and luxury of grace; and to say that we fell over head and ears in love with her would be but mild expression for our abiding emotions. We were passing through the Eden of her loveliness, and never was earthly charm more sweet than that of her caressing embraces. It was the true Tierra Caliente—the land of tropic triumph, burning beauty, passionate exhilarations!—a land which, again we say it, cannot be described even by poet's pen, because it shows the very hand and heart of Creative Love—it is *His* ageless Revelation!

From the commonest growth at our feet to the arching glory far above—Heaven's brightest carpeting all around, and springing from it in every form and hue the unstinted and unstinting life of nature, great, gorgeous blossoms, rankly richest foliage, lusciously heavy fruits—a bewildering mixture of all vegetable mystery and magical exuberance; for names were nothing—our intelligent and indefatigable guide could not begin to keep pace with our questioning, and it hardly mattered—the strangely aromatic terms passed dreamily from ear to ear, and were soon lost again in the scented distance. Only did we well remember and gladly recognize our most typical friend the palm—no longer the stunted apology of poor Atlantic or Italian coast, but a creature of plentiful and proudest prime.

And everywhere within, throughout this world of glory, moved an equal wealth and wonder of animation—birds of paradisaical hue and song, glittering insects and great palpitating lizards, large as your arm, basking by the wayside in the moist intensity of the tropic day—will you wonder, considerate reader, at our disinclination to attempt description of such a scene and experience, and will you blame us for daring to describe thus much?

Contrary to all our preconceived ideas, our manager-friend informed us that this luxuriant and often swampy region was not an unhealthy one; so, at least, he, in his several years residence and frequent hunting throughout it, had found. Of course it is not unwholesome to the natives, and we fancy almost any one could live there, in temperance, and a willingness to have the acclimating fever.

The country is full of choice game, and very fertile. Our friend told us of one immense hacienda, many leagues in extent, and stocked with many thousand brood mares. We passed near to a palatial mansion which had once been the residence of Santa Anna in his days of wealth and power, now much neglected, but still fascinating in its site by the beautiful Antigua river, and amid its tropical groves and gardens.

The villages through which our journey lay were few in number and insignificant in appearance, evidently inhabited by a poor, peasant, aboriginal population. We arrived at the half-way station (in time, not in distance, for the ascent begins shortly after leaving here) before noon, and found it to consist

HOW WE TRIED TO GET TO XALAPA.

of two or three houses, stables, etc., dignified by the poetical name of *Rinconaro*. The temperature was oppressive; we were already fatigued and half-famished, and expecting little in the way of refreshment, imagine our surprise and delight at finding a clean, cool room, spotless table-service and a delicious repast, under the cordial superintendence of a stray Frenchman, who had worthily brought the genius of his nation to bear upon the perfect profusion of the land.

So far all was well—all was more than well—our morning dream had been nothing but delight, too smooth, you will say, to last in such a land and in such times.

We had fortunately finished our repast, when our kind manager-friend entered the room, his face clouded with anxiety, and holding a mysterious dispatch in his hand. We should first mention, however, that he had before remarked upon the strangeness of the down train from Xalapa not having arrived—a most unusual occurrence, he said; he had hardly ever known it to happen in his years of managing experience. We could not proceed until its arrival, and so he had telegraphed on to know the cause of detention. The reply came couched in such ambiguous terms, that he feared mischief was brewing somewhere. We were told by the dispatch that a bridge was down near Xalapa, but to proceed at once without apprehension, etc., etc.

"Now," said Mr. T., "in my opinion this is a false statement. That bridge is not down; or if down, it never became so by fair means. Something is wrong, and with the responsibility of your safety upon my shoulders, I can only say, I fear it is the Revolution. I will proceed with you, if you like, but you must decide for yourselves; a car is at your disposal, if you conclude to return to Vera Cruz."

Here was a dilemma for a peaceable party of travellers, inoffensively longing for another look at the Mexican hills, another day or two among their contrasting charms. Shall we go on, with the risk of robbery and outrage, such as are common to Mexican life and travel, where one of the worst possibilities is the being reduced to a primeval attire—or rather a primeval absence of the same—under far from primeval conditions, or shall we act according to the better part of valor?

Under the circumstances, and finding further dispatches only deepened the mystery and increased the apprehensions of our experienced friend, who himself, however, after concealing his trusts, deemed it his duty to continue his route—with much regret we decided to return to our point of morning departure.

And now succeeded the anxiety of safe return. There seemed little doubt that the Revolution had taken possession of Xalapa, was anxious to get possession of the mails, etc., on our train, and might telegraph back to some ruffianly crew to stop and secure us before we could reach Vera Cruz again.

It was an exciting drive. Our native driver was himself aroused, and had evidently increased his emotions by internal application. His whip and voice alike lashed through the sultry tropic air, and kept our half-wild beasts at a steaming run. A number of peasant people had entered our car, and no one inspired us with much confidence but a poor foreigner, one of the employés of the line, who seemed equally anxious to reach a place of safety—so sad had been his experience in previous political upheavals of this unhappy land. Those of our party who were armed kept one hand ready, and all eyes that appreciated our peril were scanning the wayside swamps and forests, expecting every minute to see emerging from their covert a band of operatic-looking individuals, who would relieve us of all further trouble in present worldly possessions.

But, thank God! our fears were needless, though it was not till we reached Vera Cruz that night, and indeed not fully till a day or two later, that we learned of our real escape from, at the very least, a considerable annoyance. It was all true to the letter—according to the apprehensions of our sagacious friend. The Revolutionists had taken possession that morning of Xalapa, after a slight struggle; had sought to mislead us by false dispatches, but probably had not time to arrange for our capture—and thus we did *not* get to Xalapa. But do not be discouraged, friend reader; if you can go no farther, you will be more than repaid by every step of the " Caliente " way to refreshing Rinconaro.

Our Mexican notes are about finished; our few

HOW WE TRIED TO GET TO XALAPA.

more days in the country are days of waiting—waiting for the inevitable "Norther" to subside, and allow our steamer to depart. This waiting was not altogether uncomfortable, though disagreeable, from the bad drainage and frequent sand-storms of the city. Let no one tarry in its precincts longer than absolutely necessary; let him rather remain on the steamer, if possible; for the fever-fiend, we fancy, is never entirely idle in Vera Cruz.

At last we were enabled to steam away, and after the same wearisome stoppages at Mexican ports, set our prow and faces northward, only to encounter another terrible "Norther," which struck us one night like a broadside of bombs, and kept the sea, and our poor, but staunch little boat in an agony for twelve hours or more—one of those experiences from which you emerge with heart of subdued gratitude and never-ceasing wonder at the fascinated choice of those brother-beings, whose life is to 'go down to the sea in ships and to do business in great waters.'

If ever there was a motley crowd, of every social hue, from verge to verge, it was our passenger-list. Our circumscribed deck was a real stage, and on it at all hours paced and paraded the players. Not sorry were some of us to set foot again upon the soil and scope of larger acting and action, where, to say the least, there is no need of constant uncongenial jostling.

MANUEL AGUAS.

XIII.

THE CHURCH IN MEXICO.

> ———" Far away
> Tuhidthiton led forth the Aztecas,
> To spread in other lands Mexitlis' name,
> And rear a mightier empire, and set up
> Again their foul idolatry ; till Heaven,
> Making blind zeal and bloody avarice
> Its ministers of vengeance, sent among them
> The heroic Spaniards' unrelenting sword."
>
> Southey's Madoc.

THE Christian traveller in Mexico will very naturally wish to know something about the religious life of the country, convinced as he will very soon become that its only hope lies in the supremacy of a purer faith and practice.

He observes so much of ignorance and degradation in the dominant Church of Rome, the sad inheritance of a semi-barbarous conquest, which indeed was only just gilded by a pretense of conversion to the creed of a Spanish Philip and a Roman Leo.

The faith of "the Conquerors" was little better than a fetichism, a matter of miraculous madonnas and superstitious observances, with very little of Christianity's grace and truth visible in walk and conversation. Conversion consisted in persuasion or compulsion to Holy Baptism, often administered to a multitude of ignorant savages at a time. With the exception of a few great and godly men, like Las Casas, there have been very few of the Spanish Church either capable or willing to instruct and elevate the long servile and degraded masses of the people; and yet, we believe there is no aboriginal race more susceptible and prepared to receive a pure and undefiled Christianity.

The Church in Mexico received and inherited much of the worst elements of what is perhaps the worst, the least spiritual type of Romanism in Europe. There has never been anything more darkly complete than the crushing out of the Reformation in Spain. Its permission by a just and merciful God is one of the mysteries of history. The names of Ponce de la Fuente, Don Carlos de Seso, and Marina Guevera come to us from the martyr past with a fragrance of sanctity as excellent, as is the memory of Torquemada and Valdes synonymous with all that is cruelly infamous. The great crime in inquisitorial eyes was the denial of "Roman" to the Church's "Holy, Catholic" name.

A nation, a Church can give no more, no better than she has and is, and thus we have the clue to Mexico's misery. The Church of Mexico fattened upon the land. She became wealthy and overweening — like her great earthly head and centre, the enemy to all progress and enlightenment. The State, in self-defence, disestablished her, but perhaps only making her more subtly dangerous. The crisis in the religious history of Mexico seems to have occurred during the troublous times of the French attempt to seat the unfortunate Maximilian upon an imperial throne.

There must have been previously a movement of the Spirit of God in the hearts of the Mexican people, but the introduction of the Holy Scriptures and other inciting influences in those all upheaving days, seems to have first determined a renewing manifestation in the attempt of a priest named Francisco Aguilar to establish a reformed congregation. His ideas were necessarily somewhat crude and vague, but still strongly shaped in the direction of truly Catholic and Apostolic faith and service.

To strip the Church of her manifold accretions, to give her a worship understood of the people, and to afford her individual members the grace of pure Sacraments and the comfort of Holy Scripture, seems to have been the aim of this really remarkable man, for whom, however, as might be expected, the burden soon became too heavy; and when in two short years, he laid it down, let us trust, to his own eternal rest, it had already become a cross, cruelly defined, and awaiting the next hand of faith that should be strong enough to take it up.

His little flock must not be left to perish, but who shall be found competent to guide them, by GOD's grace, amid so many perils? No one had yet appeared by Aguilar's side. His battle had been fought single-handed. There is something in the wonderful discipline, or rather terrorism of Rome, which has hitherto been the greatest obstacle to anything like

THE CHURCH IN MEXICO. 131

national Church reform, and which leaves to-day the Old Catholic movement in Europe as wonderfully strong in quality as it is woefully weak in quantity.

Providentially there was at this time in New York a presbyter of the American Church, ministering to a Spanish congregation, to whom the appeal was made in behalf of this little, distant flock, and who felt it was a call of GOD too plain and potent to be disregarded. Taking his life in his hand, Dr. Henry Chauncey Riley, went in 1869 to Mexico, and set himself zealously to carry on the work of organizing a Reformed Church in that "priest-ridden" country.

His labors were blessed. He succeeded in obtaining possession of one of the principal churches in the Capital, and soon the influence of the pure cause which he represented began to make itself everywhere felt. Its greatest personal triumph was yet to come. The story of Manuel Aguas' conversion from Romanism to true Catholicism, forms one of the romantic and immortal episodes, which illumine the pages of Church History. He had been the champion of Mexican Ultramontanism, against what he had deemed a mere heretical, Protestant aggression; but a candid examination of the adversary's position led to his enlightenment, and the morning of the great field-day, on which he was to demolish, before the assembled élite of the Capital, the "pestilent" enemy's assumptions, found him instead, like his prototype, Saul of Tarsus, a most zealous preacher of the pure and undefiled Gospel and Church of Jesus Christ.

And in this new, all modifying attitude, he never wavered. He had counted the cost, and never for one moment relinquished his hold of the terrible plow, whose "share" was already—for him and for his few faithful adherents—being re-beaten into a sword of social and every martyrdom.

He became, of course, an invaluable reinforcement to the new Church, and was very soon elected its Bishop, and during the brief remainder of his life he was indefatigable in preaching, writing, teaching in every way, the truths of his utter conviction. He died, like his predecessor, Aguilar, a martyr to this all-consuming zeal; but happier than Aguilar, in leaving behind him a small but competent band of fellow-workers, who, following in his self-denying footsteps, have been blessed in the present established and most promising condition of the Reformed Church in Mexico.

The organized Synod of this Church sent a petition to the House of Bishops of the Protestant Episcopal Church in the United States, in 1874, praying for Episcopal consecration, and asserting their readiness to give all proper guarantees of Catholicity on their part. This petition was answered by the appointment of a Commission of seven Bishops, one of whom, Bishop Lee, of Delaware, went to Mexico, in 1875, and ordained several of the native candidates to the priesthood and diaconate, besides confirming a large number.

The Commission is still in sympathetic and systematizing relations with the Mexican Church, and there can be little doubt that before very long there will exist in Mexico an independent national Church, in full communion with the Reformed Catholic Church throughout the world.

In concluding this brief sketch of the religious elements in the Mexican question, almost as important and vexed a subject to the United States as is the Ultramontane problem to Europe, we feel we can do no better in pertinent, practical information and appeal, than to repeat some portions of addresses, delivered since our return home in several principal cities, in aid of our struggling sister Church.

More than two thousand miles away—beyond our own most Southern lands and seas—there lies a country, whose very name brings to the mind visions of peerless splendor and romance—a country than which Italia, with all her gift of beauty, hath no fairer bloom, and Greece, with all her song, no prouder story — a country like indeed unto that of which the prophet speaks, " a land of wheat and barley and vines and fig-trees and pomegranates—a land of oil olive and honey—a land wherein thou shalt eat bread without scarceness, thou shalt not lack anything in it."

Or—to speak with more particularity — it is a country of every capability a bountiful GOD can give, its borders laved by tropic seas, its lower regions laughing in perpetual summer, and then by grand degrees of beauty and fertility ascending into mountain summits, crowned with the glory of perpetual snows.

Within this land so gifted, lie many towns, each one of which has been the seat of independent power, as well as of marvellous advance in all the arts of life, until within the more recent centuries compelled to own the sway of mighty Anahuac, and somewhat later to exchange the feathery diadem of Montezuma for the Vice-regal crown of Cortes. This was a land, in short, of which all Europe's chivalry was dreaming, and out of which that chivalry—with its blade of many stains—carved a golden empire!

There is no need for us to inquire how much the Aztecs lost, or how little they gained by the historic exchange. We must set on the one side the bloody sacrifices of heathenism, and on the other a ruthless slavery and a cruel Inquisition. We may compare the Mexico of to-day, forever tossing on a political volcano, with the rude and rival powers of Cholula, Tlascala and Tezcuco in the days of old.

But for this we may indeed be thankful, that whether in pretence or in truth, Christ was preached by the Castilian conquerors of Mexico, and through the heavy haze of their errors and shortcomings upon the chronicling past, we may at least be thankful for the bright, immortal name of a Las Casas!

Within these latter days the light of all-reforming truth has dawned on Mexico. Out of religious despotism and social anarchy has come forth the good that the GOD of history and the Christ of liberty alone can bring!

The universal upheaval of the age—call it progress or reaction, as we will—has brought to our so-called "sister Republic" the same results, which meet the observant traveller's eye in the awakening countries of the older world—the men of the higher, educated classes, largely infidel, the women generally bigoted, the middle and lower classes somewhat indifferent, but still in the main attached to the Church from various reasons of fear or favor, while doubtless, very many even among them all have a true and lively faith in the eternal verities of Salvation, which even a papal curia cannot altogether conceal!

From these lower classes, then, to whom indeed it may be said of every land, that life brings only and ever the sternest and saddest realities—from and among the lower classes of the Mexican people has the Reformation sprung and spread.

Dissatisfied with husks, they cried for bread, and finding no response from the shepherds set over them, they appealed to GOD Himself—they have turned to us, their former "heretic" brethren and neighbors; and thus it is, Christian friends and readers, that we have the Reforming Church of Christ in Mexico asking for our sympathy and aid to-day.

I went to Mexico as a tourist, with rather indefinite ideas as to what was going on there in the way of Church revival, but with the hearty intention of finding out all I could about it in the short time of my visit.

What did I find, then, on arriving in the City of Mexico, and inquiring for the native reforming church?

I found a grand cathedral, situated in the most valuable and attractive part of the city, the very church in which the dead conqueror Cortes was laid in state, its situation a means of influence in itself, with an inviting entrance between beds of blooming flowers and tropic shrubbery, and an interior worthy of any of our own metropolitan congregations. In fine, we may say that the possession of this old historic church of San Francisco alone would give character to any movement.

Notwithstanding the cruel conscription going on at the time of our visit, which kept many of the people at home, we found a congregation fairly filling the church, and worshipping with an attention and ardor most beautiful and edifying to behold. They were the poor and the lowly of earth—those to whom and among whom the Redeemer first came, who first indeed constituted the rank and file of the Christian Church—and those, whom it is one of the saddest reflections of our Christian day, that the Church of Christ is only half able to retain. But to these devoted hearts it all seemed a tremendous and glorious reality. Their singing—the use of our own sweet hymns, such as "Jerusalem the Golden," and "Sun of my Soul," translated into most mellifluous Castilian—was one of the most impressive and touching features of worship I have ever met with in any land.

And now a word as to their clergy, with several of whom we had the great pleasure of becoming intimately acquainted. My heart glows as it recalls them one by one! Simple-hearted, lowly-minded, fervent-spirited—their demeanor and character was full of Christian sweetness and gentleness and charity. Their Bishop elect is the type of what is needed in that peculiar and exacting field—a pure-blooded Indian; this would seem an indispensable qualification of ministration to the millions of native peasant population, in whom indeed the hope of the country largely lies — a man whose every look and word of humility and faith and zeal mark him as a worthy successor to the poor, yet princely apostles of Galilee.

And his small band of clergy appeared to be generally of the same tone; one of them has been himself a Bishop-elect of the Church of Rome; another has served as an army officer, which should in itself suffice to answer for his honor, sincerity and loyalty, confirmed as it is by his venerable appearance and frank devotion. Others of them are young men, almost too young, it might seem, for such thrilling responsibilities, but apparently with an enthusiasm tempered by discretion and discipline; one or two especially struck me as men for whom, under God's provident grace, the most glowing expectations could be formed.

Going among these stranger brethren, with no claim indeed but as a presbyter of the American Church, I could not but humbly and happily feel that my Church was honored in me; and when they fell upon my neck at parting, your Christian hearts will readily understand how my own, too full for utterance, could not but most reverently though most distantly revert to that pathetic scene in early Ephesus, when the great Apostle, parting from the brethren of his love, prayed and wept with them all—"Sorrowing most of all for the words which he spake, that they should see his face no more!"

And what more shall we say of them or of their holy work? Shall we speak of their schools, which still small, on account of adverse social influences, yet proclaim the right principles and intentions of education and training? Shall we tell of the orphanage, where in a distant and secluded part of the city, alone amid inimical surroundings, a devoted Christian woman is cherishing and elevating a small band of orphans—poor little social waifs, with no one to care for them until this Church in her Master's spirit took them by the hand, clothed their bodies and warmed their hearts, and is leading them gently into and along the way of life? . . .

Of course funds are vitally needed for the relief of this Church. The clergy are poor men, who have sacrificed what little they had of temporal means and vocation, as well as of social influence and interest, in the cause of the Master Christ. Brought up as we are, with everything to favor pure and undefiled Christianity, it is almost impossible here to realize how in that benighted land a profession of Protestant or truly Catholic faith amounts to a complete ostracism—makes a social pariah of a man. Besides, their congregations, to their glory, as was said above, as also to their claim upon our Christian hearts, are the poor and lowly of earth, who, if they can keep bread in their children's mouths, the wolf from their own door, are doing well; and who can, therefore, do little for the support of those whom God has set spiritually over them.

But what we wished particularly to remark as a drawback and qualification, which should enlist our earnest sympathy and efforts, is the general ignorance and need of instruction. Belonging, as we do, to a Church which bases much of its claim upon human faith in the Catholicity of its Creeds, and the decency and order of its worship, and committed as we are to our young Mexican sister, as by the grace of God her guide and guardian in the truth, it behoves us most essentially to see that she be thoroughly instructed in the *whole* "truth as it is in Jesus," and in His "One, Holy, Catholic and Apostolic Church;" that when, by the blessing of God, she be arrived at maturity and independence of estate, we be not ashamed to point to her, and say, "Behold the sister beloved and fair, whom God gave into our fraternal hands, who is now the delight of her Divine Spouse, and a joy and comfort to the hearts of men!"

Wherefore, let our first efforts be directed towards the establishment of theological, of seminary instruction and training. We must send them translated and truly Catholic publications, those standard defenses of our Reformed faith, than which nothing can form a better and brighter weapon for their present and future need, but only such weapons of course as could be beaten into ploughshares at any moment, knowing, as we must, that the only sword which can carve its way unto the throne of the God of Love, is that forged by His Holy Spirit.

And while speaking of this essential element of love and peace in the Christian Church, we cannot forbear allusion to the humble and holy spirit of our Mexican brethren, not only towards those who with a sadly mistaken zeal have seen fit to persecute them, even "for righteousness' sake," as also towards those of their brethren of much nearer kinship, who, we deeply grieve to think, have, some of them, lost sight of the Apostolic spirit, and would apparently resolve the Apostolic work into a rival contest for spiritual supremacy. God give them soon a better mind! Surely a labor of Christian life and love such as we are fraternally interested in, which first appealed for our own immediate sympathy and succor, should be very far from suffering any let or hindrance from brethren of the same Christian home and hope, should never forcibly be made the means of presenting a divided front to the wiles and warfare of the enemy of mankind.

We have spoken of the pressing demands of this great mission work — a work so vast that in surveying its glorious possibilities, if not probabilities, the Christian eye must pass through central and southern and tropic zones, till only arrested by the silent seas that lave the furthest shores of millions lying fast bound in visible darkness — following a light once grudgingly bestowed—a light of Heaven indeed, but long hidden in such dim sanctuaries of earth that these same semi-heathen millions have only learned to groan in its glimmer!

Of such an infinite work we have sought thus imperfectly to speak, believing that, under God, this Church is called to one of the grandest tasks and responsibilities ever committed to any Communion. And we beg you to note this singular, we may, perhaps, call it *unique* fact in the history of Christian effort. *Every* cent raised, every dollar given, goes directly to the Mexican Church—goes straight to native need, to native workers in the vineyard of the Lord. We are not supporting foreign laborers, who with all their faith and zeal, must still and ever find an almost impassable gulf of national and linguistic genius between them and their infinite object. All thanks, we may add, to the signal devotion of one, who in these self-seeking days, has done so much to remind us of Apostolic example; who laying his all at the Master's feet, has gone forth to labor in a land of need, for which, indeed, by Providence of birth, and grace of gift, he seems to have been specially designated— need I say that I am most admiringly and affectionately alluding to my Right Reverend Brother elect, destined, I believe, to be known in reverent history as, under the renewing and reviving grace of Christ, one of the founders and fathers of the Reformed Church of Christ in Mexico.

APPENDIX.

SKETCH OF RECENT MEXICAN HISTORY.

The following brief summary of recent Mexican history may be of interest to the reader:

In 1821 the Independence of the country was declared.

In 1825 the first Congress assembled.

In 1836 Santa Anna was made President, and deprived of office in the same year.

In 1838, another Revolution; blockade of Vera Cruz by the French, who are driven off by the energetic Santa Anna. After one or two revolutions he is declared Dictator, in 1841.

In 1843, after another revolution, a new and entirely intolerant Constitution is adopted.

In 1846, after several years' turbulent history, in which Santa Anna plays the principal part, a war is begun with the United States.

In 1848, the war closes with Santa Anna's defeat, and peace is concluded with the United States.

In 1853, after several more revolutions, Santa Anna turns up again as Dictator, but is obliged to resign the next year.

In 1856 begins a strong movement against the Church, under Comonfort, who becomes President, and effects the sequestration of church property. He is not long in power.

In 1859, the famous Miramon appears for a brief period as President, and reappears at the head of the Church party, in 1860, to make way the next year for the liberal President, and afterwards Dictator Juarez.

Then came the French invasion, terminated in 1867 by the execution of Maximilian and the undisputed sway of Juarez, who at his death is succeeded by Lerdo, the present occupant of this most unsteady seat of power being Diaz.

EXPENSE OF A TRIP TO MEXICO.

There are excursion tickets issued by the Alexandre Steamer line in New York, to Vera Cruz and back, for $150; or you take rail to New Orleans and purchase an excursion ticket there, the latter costing $100 in gold. Or again, one can take a steamer to Havana, and thence proceed by a French Messagerie boat, or an English mail-steamer to Vera Cruz. First class fare from Vera Cruz to the City of Mexico, $16. Comfortable lodgings and board can be obtained in the capital for $2 or $3 a day, from which few data an estimate for the whole trip can easily be made.

For further valuable practical information, see "Ferguson's Anecdotical Guide to Mexico," recently published.

www.ingramcontent.com/pod-product-compliance
Lightning Source LLC
Chambersburg PA
CBHW030345170426
43202CB00010B/1249